THE BEST HITS ON THE
BLUES
HIGHWAY

THE BEST HITS ON THE

BLUES

HIGHWAY

NASHVILLE TO NEW ORLEANS ON ROUTE 61

AMY BIZZARRI

Globe
Pequot
ESSEX, CONNECTICUT

Globe
Pequot

An imprint of Globe Pequot, the trade division of
The Rowman & Littlefield Publishing Group, Inc.
4501 Forbes Blvd., Ste. 200
Lanham, MD 20706
www.rowman.com

Distributed by NATIONAL BOOK NETWORK

British Library Cataloguing in Publication Information available

Library of Congress Cataloging-in-Publication Data

Names: Bizzarri, Amy, author.
Title: The best hits on the Blues Highway : Nashville to New Orleans on
   Route 61 / Amy Bizzarri.
Other titles: Nashville to New Orleans on Route 61
Description: Essex, Connecticut : Globe Pequot, [2024] | Includes index.
Identifiers: LCCN 2023046901 (print) | LCCN 2023046902 (ebook) | ISBN
   9781493078462 (paperback) | ISBN 9781493078479 (ebook)
Subjects: LCSH: United States Highway 61—Guidebooks. | Southern
   States—Guidebooks. | Musical landmarks—Southern States—Guidebooks. |
   Music museums—Southern States—Guidebooks. | Automobile
   travel—Southern States—Guidebooks.
Classification: LCC F207.3 .B59 2024 (print) | LCC F207.3 (ebook) | DDC
   917.604—dc23/eng/20231108
LC record available at https://lccn.loc.gov/2023046901
LC ebook record available at https://lccn.loc.gov/2023046902

A

follow up to
I FALL TO PIECES
from

PATSY CLINE

"CRAZY"
c/w
"WHO CAN I COUNT ON"

31317

"LIFE IS LIKE A TRUMPET -
if you don't put anything into it,
you don't get anything out of it.
WILLIAM CHRISTOPHER HANDY

**"Everything comes out in Blues music:
JOY, PAIN, STRUGGLE.** Blues
is affirmation with absolute elegance.
WYNTON MARSALIS

CONTENTS

INTRODUCTION

FROM JAZZ TO BLUEGRASS TO BLUES TO ROCK 'N ROLL TO RAP, music has always been the backdrop of U.S. history, expressing what it means to be American. Our melting pot of a nation—or better, mixing bowl—is rich with the traditions and talents that combined to create the soundtrack of the American experience.

This road trip guide will take you through our nation's history through music.

Your musical journey begins in Nashville, Tennessee, the city that "music calls home," and ends in New Orleans, the birthplace of jazz.

Interstate 40 connects Nashville to Memphis, where so many music legends found their footing or simply struck a chord in the city's juke joints, nightclubs, and bars, while Stax Records and Sun Studio recorded the hits that would change the tune of America into history.

Highway 61 ushers motorists through the Mississippi Delta, "The Most Southern Place on Earth," where the blues was born, inspired by the highs and lows of life, the triumphs, the struggles, the great loves, and the loves lost. As you drive along Route 61, you'll pass railroads, rivers, fields, and slaughterhouses. People in these modest locations expressed themselves with melancholy "blue" tones and candid lyrics beginning at the dawn of the twentieth century, revolutionizing the world of music in this region—now widely considered the cradle of American culture. Still today, its music culture shines as contemporary musicians carry on the legacy of the great Delta Blues artists of yesteryear.

Though the itinerary highlights the most important historic, music-related sites easily accessible from the route that runs from Nashville to New Orleans, and along the legendary Blues Highway, Route 61, through the Mississippi Delta, it also veers off course to experience lesser-known sights and sounds. Beyond the curated list of the most iconic sights to see on this musical journey, expect to discover hidden gems. As you set off on the musical journey of a lifetime, buckle up and turn your radio volume up to the max to blast the hits that made America.

YOUR PLAYLIST FOR A ROCKIN' ROAD TRIP

Scan the QR code to hear a Spotify playlist with over 100 songs created by the music icons featured in this travel guide.

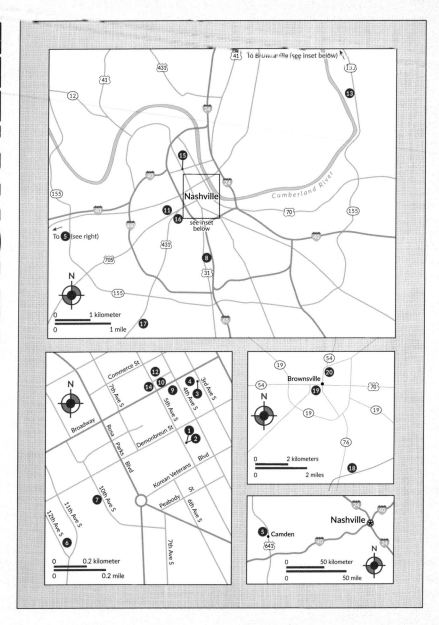

1. Country Music Hall of Fame and Museum

2. Hatch Show Print

3. Johnny Cash Museum

4. Patsy Cline Museum

5. Patsy Cline Plane Crash Site Memorial

6. Bluegrass Jam at the Station Inn

7. The Gibson Garage

8. Gruhn Guitars

9. Nudie's Honky Tonk

10. Tootsie's Orchid Lounge

11. White Limozeen

12. Ryman Auditorium

13. Grand Ole Opry Live

14. National Museum of African American Music

15. The Historic Center of Nashville's African American Community

16. RCA Studio B

17. Bluebird Cafe

18. Tina Turner's Schoolhouse and the home of "Sleepy" John Adam Estes

19. Billy Tripp's Mindfield

20. Helen's BBQ

To me, songwriting is the backbone of Nashville.
Looks can go, fads can go, but
A GOOD SONG LASTS FOREVER.
ALAN JACKSON

♪ COUNTRY MUSIC HALL OF FAME AND MUSEUM
"THE HOUSE THAT HOLDS THE MUSIC"

FOR A COUNTRY MUSIC ARTIST, becoming a member of the Country Music Hall of Fame is the highest honor in the genre.

Every year since 1961, the Country Music Association (CMA) inducts a select number of performers, songwriters, broadcasters, musicians, and executives into the exclusive Hall of Fame as a way to highlight significant contributions to the development of country music. The first inductees were Jimmie Rodgers, Fred Rose, and Hank Williams; since then, over 150 members have been added to the official roster of the coveted club. Bas-relief bronze plaques depicting each inductee hang in the grand rotunda of the Country Music Hall of Fame and Museum, a massive, bass clef–shaped museum in the heart of downtown Nashville. This vibrant museum, the repository of one of the world's most extensive musical collections, tells the tale of country music through priceless sheet music, songbooks, costumes, vehicles, musical instruments, original recordings, photographs, archival video, and the building itself.

Can you spot hidden musical details concealed in the museum's unique exterior architecture? The front windows represent piano keys. The diamond-shaped tower that caps the rotunda is a replica of the circa 1932 broadcast antenna of Nashville-based country music station WSM. The sweeping arch that ends at an angle on the right side of the building mimics the fin of a 1950s-era Cadillac. The four disc-shaped tiers on the rooftop represent the evolution of recording technology, from the humble 78, to the vinyl LP, to the 45, and last but not least, the compact disc. Even the materials used to build the museum are symbolic—wood, concrete, steel, and stone—construction elements native to the geographic home of country music, the Mid-South.

Special exhibits shine a spotlight on stars of the past and present. Among the museum's more than 2.5 million precious artifacts, which include over 900 musical instruments, see if you can spot Mother Maybelle Carter's Gibson L-5 guitar; Patsy Cline's cowgirl costume designed and sewed by her mother, Hilda Hensley; "The Log," one of the first solid body electric guitars built, the brainchild of jazz guitarist Les Paul; Bob Wills' fiddle; and Gram Parsons' rhinestone-encrusted "Nudie suit." Two automobiles on display encapsulate their drivers' style: Webb Pierce's flashy 1962 Pontiac Bonneville that Nudie Cohn (see page 14) bedazzled with silver dollars and equipped with a pistol door handle, and Elvis Presley's 1960 "Solid Gold" Cadillac limousine.

The museum's most hallowed space is the soaring rotunda, where the Hall of Fame members' plaques on display recall musical notes. The title of the song "Will the Circle Be Unbroken" circles the interior of the rotunda. That same song, which symbolizes the (musical) bond that connects past and present, is traditionally played by new and old Hall of Fame members at the close of the annual induction ceremony.

222 5th Ave. South, Nashville; countrymusichalloffame.org

HATCH SHOW PRINT

Hatch Show Print posters once served as the visual advertising medium for musicians looking to promote upcoming shows. Since 1879, the letterpress print shop has been cranking out limited-run posters, designed and printed in-house with vintage wood type, showcasing upcoming concerts from every musical artist under the Mid-South sun. Once located in downtown Nashville, the entire shop moved into the Country Music Hall of Fame and Museum in 2013, continuing its precious handmade tradition. Take the backstage tour of Hatch Show Print to smell the ink, handle the wood-type letters, and see how presses churn out such iconic posters, or take a workshop to make a poster print of your very own.

222 5th Avenue South, Nashville; countrymusichalloffame.org

Lou Stejskal

♪ JOHNNY CASH MUSEUM

ALL YOUR LIFE, YOU WILL BE FACED WITH A CHOICE. YOU CAN CHOOSE LOVE OR HATE . . . I CHOOSE LOVE. —JOHNNY CASH

BORN INTO A FAMILY OF poor cotton farmers in Kingsland, Arkansas, Johnny Cash became one of the best-selling recording artists ever. Raised on gospel music, he began playing and writing songs at the age of twelve before recording the multi-genre music that made him a legend. Cash embraced country, rockabilly, blues, rock 'n roll, and gospel, all in his signature, deep, calm bass-baritone voice, often to train-like, chugging guitar rhythms. His trademark nickname—The Man in Black— came from his somber, all-black performance wardrobe. Though he was known for his rebellious nature, he traditionally began his concerts with the same humble introduction: "Hello, I'm Johnny Cash."

The Johnny Cash Museum in downtown Nashville houses the world's most extensive collection of Johnny Cash artifacts. Exhibits are arranged in chronological order, highlighting Cash's journey from challenging childhood—through artifacts such as bags of cotton, his family's home piano, and school report cards—to star—attested by the many gold and platinum records and Grammy and CMA awards on display.

The "Progression of Sound" exhibit highlights Cash's lifelong experimentation with genres of music and recording media, and a Sun Records exhibit shines a spotlight on the Memphis label that helped launch his career into the stratosphere. Clips of Cash's many television appearances are screened in another exhibit space: Cash not only hosted his own variety television show with his wife June Carter Cash by his side but also starred as a guest character on television shows *Little House on the Prairie*, *Dr. Quinn, Medicine Woman*, and *Hee Haw*.

Cash threaded a folded dollar bill through the strings of his Martin guitar to mimic a percussion sound in the years before he had a drummer; that same guitar is on display, along with his first gold record, "I Walk the Line."

Perhaps the most poignant artifact in the museum is the handwritten lyrics from the last song he wrote, days before his death, "Like the 309."

"I love songs about horses, railroads, land, Judgment Day, family, hard times, whiskey, courtship, marriage, adultery, separation, murder, war, prison, rambling, damnation, home, salvation, death, pride, humor, piety, rebellion, patriotism, larceny, determination, tragedy, rowdiness, heartbreak and love. And Mother. And God," explained Johnny Cash. "Like the 309" is about a train journey to heaven.

Touring this self-guided museum takes about an hour. As a memento, pose in front of the green screen to take a photo with a (virtual) Cash.

119 3rd Ave. South, Nashville; johnnycashmuseum.com

♪ PATSY CLINE MUSEUM
IF YOU CAN'T DO IT WITH FEELING—DON'T. —PATSY CLINE

PATSY CLINE WAS A TOUGH YET TENDER TRAILBLAZER with a soothing, expressive contralto voice who made an indelible mark on music. One of the first country performers to cross over into pop music, Cline is credited as a creator of the Nashville sound: pop-infused country music. She was also the first country singer to headline her own show in Las Vegas and the first woman in country music to perform at New York's Carnegie Hall, though she noted, "Carnegie Hall was real fabulous, but you know, it ain't as big as the Grand Ole Opry."

Born Virginia Patterson Hensley on September 8, 1932, in Winchester, Virginia, Cline overcame endless obstacles throughout her short life.

At age thirteen, a bout of rheumatic fever stopped her heartbeat for a spell. "You might say it was my return to the living after several days that launched me as a singer," Cline said. "The fever affected my throat, and when I recovered, I had this booming voice like Kate Smith's."

At twenty-nine, just as her songs were climbing the charts, she was almost killed in a head-on car collision that tossed her through a

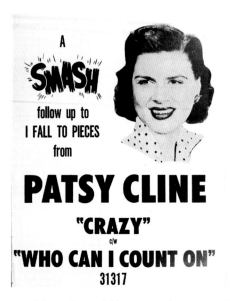

A **SMASH** follow up to I FALL TO PIECES from

PATSY CLINE

"CRAZY"

c/w

"WHO CAN I COUNT ON"

31317

windshield. Ever determined, Cline refused to let her injuries slow her down: Still on crutches, she performed at the Grand Ole Opry's stage to sing her biggest hit yet: "I recorded a song called 'I Fall to Pieces' and I was in a car wreck. Now I'm worried because I have a brand-new record, and it's called 'Crazy'!"

"Crazy" would become the most-played jukebox record of all time.

Cline began performing as a child, partly because she loved to sing but also to help support her family after her father left when she was a young teen. She debuted wearing cutesy cowgirl outfits her mother sewed, and she taught herself to play the piano. When she was about fourteen, she showed up at her local radio station, WINC, and boldly asked radio DJ Joltin' Jim McCoy if she could audition. "Well, if you've got nerve enough to stand before that mic and sing over the air live," he said, "I've got nerve enough to let you."

By her early twenties, Cline was on her way toward country music stardom. She first recorded on the Four Star label in 1955. She embraced radio and television with appearances on a local variety show, *Town and Country Jamboree*, followed by Arthur Godfrey's *Talent Scouts*, which gave her nationwide exposure, before becoming a regular performer on the ultimate radio show, the *Grand Ole Opry*. Her signature song "I Fall to Pieces" topped the charts for thirty-nine consecutive weeks and was the first of several hit country-pop crossovers.

At the height of her stardom, Cline began experiencing premonitions of her own death, and reportedly told singer Ray Walker, "Honey, I've had two bad ones [accidents]. The third one will either be a charm, or it'll kill me."

On March 5, 1963, she was proved right. After playing a benefit concert in Kansas City, Cline was en route to Nashville with her manager and fellow country music stars Hawkshaw Hawkins and Cowboy Copas, when her plane, a tiny Piper PA-24, nose-dived at full speed into the Tennessee wilderness. Cline was just thirty.

Among the many mementos on display in the intimate Patsy Cline Museum, perhaps the most poignant are the sewing machine used by Cline's mother, Hilda Hensley, to sew her signature cowgirl costumes; her salt and pepper shaker collection; and her signature boot-shaped cigarette lighter. But it's the re-creations of rooms from the modest, midcentury modern Nashville home she shared with her husband Charlie Dick that bring her story and warmth back to life. Dick saved as many

PATSY CLINE PLANE CRASH SITE MEMORIAL

Deep in the middle of the woods, the Patsy Cline Plane Crash Site Memorial, an engraved boulder, marks where Patsy Cline's life tragically ended in a plane crash.
The small, adjacent gazebo features a collage of Cline's life and is the perfect place to sit and reflect.

2082 Mount Carmel Rd., Camden, TN

memories as he could of his cherished wife, even Cline's still-running Norge refrigerator, a canceled check used to pay the deposit for the furniture in her home, and her Jimmy Dean fan club card.

Perhaps the most moving memento on display is the wristwatch Patsy Cline wore when the private plane she was traveling on crashed that terrible evening, its hands stopped at 6:20, the moment of impact.

"When the family found all of Patsy's things that Charlie Dick had saved, it makes me believe that this museum was meant to be," said museum founder Bill Miller.

119 3rd Ave. South, Nashville; patsymuseum.com

♪ BLUEGRASS JAM AT THE STATION INN
BEST BLUEGRASS IN THE WORLD

NEARLY EVERY NIGHT OF THE YEAR SINCE 1974, the bluegrass beat reverberates throughout the Station Inn in Nashville's Gulch neighborhood. With every seat in this small listening room near enough to the stage to see the sweat and feel the notes sing from the instruments, this is as close as you can come to the best bluegrass in the world. Some of the biggest names in the bluegrass biz have graced the Station Inn stage—Ricky Skaggs, Jerry Douglas, Alison Krauss, Peter Rowan, Sam Bush, Curly Seckler, Jimmy Martin, Bobby Osborne, and Bill Monroe, the so-called Father of Bluegrass—and stars pop in on occasion, hiding among the audience after performing at the Grand Ole Opry on a Friday or Saturday night.

The bluegrass style was born in the southern Appalachian Mountains and likely borrowed its name from Kentucky bluegrass, a smooth meadow grass that often appears blue-green under the sun. American mandolinist,

singer, and songwriter Bill Monroe, who hailed from Kentucky, aka the Bluegrass State, and his nascent Bill Monroe & the Blue Grass Boys, were the first to include all the elements that set bluegrass music apart from older string-band music: syncopated, high-energy rhythm; tight, sophisticated vocal harmony; "breaks" or solos on the mandolin, banjo, and fiddle; lyrics that range from playful to poignant; and a strong influence of jazz and blues. Bluegrass emphasizes the off-beat, though notes are anticipated, separating it from the laid-back blues where notes are behind the beat.

Originally located near Centennial Park, the intimate venue was founded by a group of six bluegrass pickers and grew along with bluegrass itself. By the time the Station Inn moved to its present location

In the Gulch, near Music Row, in 1978, it had become the unofficial gathering place of the genre.

Every Sunday at 7 p.m., the Station hosts a bluegrass jam, a classic picking circle wherein all musicians sit in the round and play together. Anyone who wants to observe is seated outside the circle. Only bluegrass instruments—fiddle, banjo, mandolin, acoustic guitar, dobro, and double bass—are allowed. There's no skill level required to participate, so even beginners might find themselves picking along with a living legend of bluegrass.

Jam admission is free and first come, first served, but, with just 200 seats, it tends to fill up. More seating often opens up at intermission, around 10:15 p.m. The bar opens with the door about two hours before showtime, so settle into your seat and dig into pizza, nachos, chips and salsa, popcorn, Daddy Bob's pimento, GooGoo Clusters, or Moon Pies with cocktails or craft beer.

402 12th Ave. South, Nashville; stationinn.com

♪ THE GIBSON GARAGE
THE ULTIMATE GUITAR EXPERIENCE

GUITAR BRAND GIBSON HAS BEEN GIVING MUSICIANS the means to create their magic for more than a century. Founded in 1894, Gibson, maker of acoustic and electric guitars, mandolins, and banjos, is beloved around the world for its pioneering designs and user-friendly yet alluring aesthetic. Gibson's flagship store in Nashville, the Gibson Garage, is a must-visit destination for players and music lovers alike.

Orville H. Gibson was a luthier, a craftsperson who builds and repairs string instruments, working in the late nineteenth century in Kalamazoo,

Michigan, when he invented a ten-string mandolin-guitar and his signature violin-inspired guitar with a curved top and bottom, and sides carved (not bent or pressed) into shape. He applied for a patent for his designs, and the brand was born. Gibson's guitars and mandolins played louder and were more durable than contemporary instruments, and musicians flocked to his one-room workshop.

The Gibson brand has continued to make and market innovative stringed instruments well beyond Orville's death in 1918. As the guitar grew in popularity, so did Gibson. Gibson introduced its first electric guitar, the ES-150, aka the "Electric Spanish" in 1936. The "Les Paul" guitar, named after the pioneering jazz, country, and blues guitarist, was introduced in 1952. The slimmer Thinline series was introduced in the mid-1950s. The modernistic Explorer and Flying V arrived on the scene in 1958, followed by the Firebird in the early 1960s. In the 1970s, Gibson relocated its operations from Kalamazoo to Nashville, aka Music City, USA.

The 8,000-square-foot Gibson Garage, located in downtown Nashville, is the flagship and carries its entire range of brands, including Epiphone and Kramer, Mesa Boogie, and KRK. Experts here can help you find your next guitar or repair your beloved instrument at the on-site

Repair and Restoration Center. At the in-store Custom Shop, players can select their wood, finish, pickups, and knobs, and Gibson's expert luthiers will create (or re-create) the customized guitar of their dreams. And a small stage hosts an array of live concerts.

If you're interested in music history, check out the exhibit that displays beautiful instruments handcrafted by founder Orville Gibson, including an intricately carved guitar with an ornate butterfly inlay that he crafted in 1900.

209 10th Ave. South, Nashville; gibson.com

♪ GRUHN GUITARS

GRUHN GUITARS HAS BEEN buying, selling, trading, and appraising vintage guitars, basses, banjos, mandolins, ukuleles, and amps since 1970. George Gruhn, an expert on vintage American guitars, opened the first store at 111 4th Avenue North with an inventory of twenty-two instruments; today, Gruhn's 8th Avenue South location houses more than 1,100 instruments, making it one of the world's largest collections of premier vintage and used guitars.

2120 8th Ave. South, Nashville; guitars.com

♪ NUDIE'S HONKY TONK
LIVIN' THE (RHINESTONE-BEDAZZLED) AMERICAN DREAM

NUDIE COHN LIVED AND BREATHED the American dream. He worked his way up from a shoeshine boy to a boxer to a sought-after costume designer. His flamboyant, rhinestone-bedazzled "Nudie suits" were worn by celebrities across the spectrum of style. Elvis Presley, Hank Williams, Gram Parsons, John Wayne, Cher, Ronald Reagan, ZZ Top, Elton John,

Porter Wagoner, Robert Mitchum, Glen Campbell, the Monkees . . . all strutted their stuff onstage or on-screen in a signature, always over-the-top "Nudie suit."

Originally named Nuta Kotlyarenko, he was born to a Ukrainian Jewish family in Kiev, Ukraine, in 1902, a time when ethnic Jews were regularly subjected to pogroms—violent, mob-like massacres officially mandated by the local Russian authorities. By 1921, an estimated 100,000 Jewish people were killed, maimed, or tortured in pogroms in Ukraine.

Nuta Kotlyarenko's parents rightfully feared for their lives. So they made the heart-wrenching decision to send eleven-year-old Nuta and his brother Julius off on a ship bound for New York City.

Young Nuta earned his living as a shoeshine boy, and later as a boxer. He soon married, and Nuta and his wife Helen supplemented their income by creating costumes and undergarments for strippers and showgirls, "Nudie's for the Ladies." No one knows exactly if Nuta changed his name to Nudie on his own, or if his name was a typo at the Ellis Island immigrant register, but no one could argue that the name fit Cohn's early career to a tee.

Country music star Tex Williams gave Nudie the nudge to start Nudie's Rodeo Tailors. Williams, early in his career, wanted glitzy suits, but they were too expensive for the rising star. Legend states that in 1947, Williams sold a horse to fund Nudie's first sewing machine so the tailor could make the singer's stage suits at a price that fit his small costume budget. Williams became a singing advertisement for Nudie, and soon Cohn sold his signature suits at "Nudie's of Hollywood," on the corner of Victory Boulevard and Vineland Avenue in North Hollywood.

Nudie suits weren't just suits; they were spectacular statement pieces. Perhaps most famous was the $10,000 gold lamé Nudie suit worn

by singer Elvis Presley on the cover of his 1959 hit album, *50,000,000 Elvis Fans Can't Be Wrong*.

Nudie's Honky Tonk, Nashville's largest honky tonk, is a mini museum dedicated to the inventive, over-the-top costume designer. In addition to live music, cold beer, cocktails, and Southern-style comfort food, the century-old three-story former Lawrence Records Building showcases Nudie's glitziest suits. It is also home to the longest bar in Music City; at over 100 feet, the bar shines with more than 10,000 embedded silver dollars.

Cohn also loved to customize cars: He silver-dollar-studded their

> **Some people tap their feet, some people snap their fingers, and some people sway back and forth. I JUST SORTA DO 'EM ALL TOGETHER, I GUESS.**
>
> ELVIS, IN 1956, TALKING ABOUT
> HIS WAY OF MOVING ONSTAGE

dashboards, swapped door handles and gear shifts for silver pistols, and added longhorn steer horns to the hood. Nudie's modified Cadillac El Dorado, also known as the "Nudie Mobile," is mounted on the wall and is protected with a $400,000 insurance policy.

And though Nudie's suits appear all-American, they also share some details characteristic of traditional Ukrainian style where men's and women's shirts typically feature colorful, symbolic embroidery. Cohn usually wore mismatched boots to remind himself of his humble origins in Ukraine, when his family couldn't afford a matching pair of shoes for him.

409 Broadway, Nashville; nudieshonkytonk.com

♪ TOOTSIE'S ORCHID LOUNGE
MORE THAN A HONKY TONK

IN 1960, HATTIE LOUISE "TOOTSIE" BESS bought a bar named Mom's. Looking to freshen up the dingy exterior, Tootsie hired a painter. One day she arrived at her bar to find that he had painted it a bright, rich purple, the color of orchids in bloom. Tootsie switched the name to "Tootsie's Orchid Lounge," and a legend was officially born.

With just an alley separating the back door of Tootsie's from the stage door of the Ryman Auditorium, the original home of the Grand Ole Opry, Tootsie's was a welcoming bar where up-and-coming stars could catch a breath of air between sets. The Ryman was made to house a gospel tabernacle, not a musical variety show, and it lacked a proper backstage area, with a single dressing room for the men (women were relegated to an inadequate ladies' restroom). So Tootsie's became the unofficial backstage area. Tootsie herself was more than a honky tonk proprietor: She was a therapist, a cheerleader, a booking agent, a microloan agent, and a beacon of kindness to the thousands of singers, songwriters, and musicians who considered Tootsie's their home away from home. She collected the photos of the stars she came to love and proudly framed and displayed them on the walls (today's Tootsie's Wall of Fame).

Tootsie had a knack for spotting talent, and she hired aspiring artists to work the bar, sometimes slipping cash into their pockets or lending them money when she knew they were in need. American singer, songwriter, and actor Kris Kristofferson called Tootsie's "a home for homeless souls."

Willie Nelson got his first songwriting job after singing onstage here. "Nashville was a struggle," Nelson told *The Guardian* in May 2015. "I moved there in 1960, at about the time I turned 27 . . . I was as broke as the Ten Commandments. When a cold front hit Nashville that winter, I sat at the bar at Tootsie's and gazed out the window, watching the drifting snow, feeling as low as low can be. . . . The world took a turn, as it always will, and a week later, I was back at Tootsie's. I brought my guitar and welcomed what songwriters called a pulling: That's when we trot out our songs and play 'em for each other. The mood was a mix of friendly competition and brotherly support. The songwriters included guys like Hank Cochran, Harlan Howard, Mel Tillis, and Roger Miller. I felt lucky to be in their company. Hank, who was selling songs, treated me like a winner. 'You'll make money at this, Willie,' he said. 'You're too good not to.' He told me about a music publishing firm and, a few days later, drove me to play my songs for the head honcho, Hal Smith. I trotted out my best stuff—'Night Life,' 'Crazy,' 'Funny How Time Slips Away.' 'Sounds good,' was all Smith said. 'Let me get back to you.' Wasn't 24 hours later that Hank came back to the trailer park. 'You're hired,' he said. 'How does 50 bucks a week sound?' Sounded great. My first job as a professional songwriter."

When Dolly Parton moved to Nashville the day after her high school graduation in 1964, Tootsie's was one of the first places she performed.

"Just about everybody who has played the Opry has put in some time at Tootsie's," Parton said on a 1987 episode of *The Dolly Show*. "Even if you don't drink, there's some pretty potent conversation. It's always been a place where singers and songwriters like to hang out. One thing everybody who came to Tootsie's had in common was a head full of dreams. You can tell by the pictures on the wall the dreams do come true. Dreams are nothin' without hard work and determination to back them up. And it sure helps to have people who believe in you."

Tootsie passed away in 1978 and was laid to rest in an orchid gown in an orchid-colored casket. Country music legend Connie Smith sang some of Tootsie's favorite hymns to the family members, friends, musicians, and songwriters attending her funeral.

Tootsie's is still a vibrant honky tonk, packed every night of the week, with live bands playing on the first and second floors and third-floor patio.

"The artists just loved Mrs. Tootsie, because she would take care of them," said John Taylor, the current entertainment director at Tootsie's. "We call Tootsie's 'honky tonk boot camp.' We know that a lot of the kids come to get started here. . . . It's fun working with them and carrying on a tradition that Tootsie got started."

422 Broadway, Nashville; tootsies.net

WHITE LIMOZEEN

The Graduate Nashville's White Limozeen rooftop bar is a glorious tribute to Dolly Parton. Named after her 1989 album of the same name, which features a country girl living an opulent lifestyle, the decor and menu at the White Limozeen match her sparkling personality. The poolside furniture is covered in pink roses and shaded by pink-fringe umbrellas, and the menu features caviar, champagne jello shots, and a "millionaire's Twinkie." A giant Dolly sculpture watches over the always-animated scene.

101 20th Ave. North, Nashville; graduatehotels.com

♪ RYMAN AUDITORIUM
THE MOTHER CHURCH OF COUNTRY MUSIC

THE *GRAND OLE OPRY* RADIO SHOW is the longest-running radio program in the United States. When it debuted in 1925, it could be heard by listeners across thirty states. When fans began arriving at the doorstep of Nashville's WSM studio to catch the show as it was recorded live, the WSM Barn Dance, as it was initially called, realized they needed a bigger venue. After trying several smaller venues, the Grand Ole Opry moved to the Ryman Auditorium on June 5, 1943, where it hosted countless sold-out shows and stars galore for over thirty-one years, earning its nickname "The Mother Church of Country Music."

Before it was the home of the Grand Ole Opry, the Ryman was a house of worship, the Union Gospel Tabernacle, built by Thomas Ryman in 1892.

Ryman, who owned a waterfront saloon and a fleet of riverboats, attended a tent revival led by the South's most famous preacher in the late nineteenth century, Samuel Porter Jones, in 1886, intending to heckle the evangelist offstage. Jones, who aimed his direct and sometimes coarse sermons at men, preached, among other things, that alcohol was sinful—a belief that wasn't in line with saloon proprietor Ryman's convictions. But Jones managed to convert Ryman, who pledged to use his fortune to build a tabernacle so that others might experience the same miracle.

Though it boasts decidedly church-like details such as stained-glass windows and pew seating, the Tabernacle, beyond revivals, funded its operations by hosting everything from boxing matches to concerts (the Fisk Jubilee Singers debuted onstage here in 1892) to presentations (by famous figures including Booker T. Washington, Helen Keller, and Harry Houdini).

When Ryman died in 1904, an estimated four thousand people attended his funeral at the Tabernacle on Christmas day. Reverend Jones spoke at the service and proposed changing the Tabernacle's name to the Ryman Auditorium in his honor.

The *Grand Ole Opry* went national in 1927, when it was scheduled to follow NBC's *Music Appreciation Hour*, a radio broadcast devoted to classical music. Host George Hay inadvertently gave the show its name when he noted the contrast of the stuffy, lyrical opera in the preceding show to the rollicking performance of "Harmonica Wizard" DeFord Bailey, the first artist to appear on the nationwide broadcast: "Well, we'd just heard the grand old opera, so let's now turn to the Grand Ole Opry for us regular folks."

The careers of countless country music legends—Roy Acuff, Hank Williams, Patsy Cline, Loretta Lynn, Johnny Cash, Minnie Pearl—were launched here at the Ryman, voices bolstered by the auditorium's incredible acoustics. But by 1974, the show had outgrown its historic home and moved to the 4,000-seat Grand Ole Opry House northeast of downtown.

The best way to experience one of the most revered music venues in the United States is to catch a live show; check www.ryman.com/events to reserve tickets for upcoming performances. The Ryman Auditorium also offers guided tours that will bring you backstage and even onstage, where you can snap a selfie as you sing your heart out in the Mother Church of Country Music.

116 5th Ave. North, Nashville; ryman.com

GRAND OLE OPRY LIVE

Join in the fun by attending one of the *Grand Ole Opry*'s live broadcasts at its latest, larger home. Every show features live performances by eight or more stellar musicians, plus surprise guests and collaborations.

2804 Opryland Dr., Nashville; opry.com

♪ NATIONAL MUSEUM OF AFRICAN AMERICAN MUSIC

CELEBRATING THE BELOVED MUSICAL GENRES CREATED, INFLUENCED, AND INSPIRED BY AFRICAN AMERICANS

RAGTIME, ROCK 'N ROLL, RAP, funk, jazz, blues, hip hop, gospel, and R&B. . . . African Americans have played a central role in shaping and creating all genres of American music. The National Museum of African American Music, which opened in 2017, is the only museum in the United States dedicated to preserving the legacy of the fifty-plus musical genres created, influenced, and inspired by African Americans. In an interview with CBS News about the museum, Grammy Award–winning singer and songwriter Gabriella Sarmiento Wilson (known professionally as H.E.R.) said, "There would be no Elvis without Chuck Berry; there would be no Led Zeppelin, Beatles, or country music without the blues."

"African American music is American music," said John Fleming, the museum's immediate past director. "Early white historians believed that Africans arrived in the Americas without culture. We now know that they brought with them a rich cultural heritage that would become central to the development of American culture."

Courtesy of National Museum of African American Music

The experience begins in the Roots Theater, where a brief film highlights the rich history of Black music in America. Six galleries guide visitors through American music history, starting with the Rivers of Rhythm corridor, where an animated timeline takes visitors across the ages through music. At the Wade in the Water gallery, which documents the influence of indigenous African music and the formation of African American spirituals and hymns, visitors are invited to record themselves singing live with a gospel choir. The Crossroads gallery chronicles the blues, from the work songs sung by sharecroppers to the songs born of the Great Migration. The Love Supreme gallery explores jazz and the various musical styles it inspired, including Dixieland, swing, bebop, cool, hard bop, and fusion.

Moving closer to the present day, the One Nation Under a Groove gallery documents the history of R&B, which emerged after World War II. One Nation Under a Groove brings *Soul Train* to life; visitors can produce their own original songs and participate in a virtual dance battle. The Revolutionary Power of Hip Hop explores the messages behind top rap and hip hop hits, and visitors can produce their own original beats.

The National Museum of African American Music is more than a museum: It's a highly immersive experience. Request a radio frequency identification (RFID) bracelet for a nominal fee, and as you move through the museum, hold your RFID bracelet over each interactive station's sensors to save playlists, videos, and more. Download your media at home for a musical souvenir.

510 Broadway, Nashville; nmaam.org

♪ THE HISTORIC CENTER OF NASHVILLE'S AFRICAN AMERICAN COMMUNITY

THE INTERSECTION OF Rosa Parks Boulevard and Jefferson Street is the historic center of Nashville's African American community. This area is home to three historically Black universities: Fisk University, Meharry Medical College, and Tennessee State University. Many of the sit-ins—peaceful protests to end racial segregation in the 1960s—took place at lunch counters located here in this corner of downtown Nashville. Music icons including Marvin Gaye, Otis Redding, Aretha Franklin, and Jimi Church performed at the many clubs along Jefferson Street. The Jefferson Street Sound Museum is dedicated to preserving the musical history of the historic neighborhood. It houses a music production studio and rehearsal hall while showcasing art and artifacts that recall the days when music flowed from the many area clubs.

2004 Jefferson St., Nashville; jeffersonstreetsound.com

♪ RCA STUDIO B
"TEMPLE OF SOUND"

IF THESE WALLS COULD TALK, THEY'D SING. The voices of so many legends have echoed in this small space, built in 1957 according to plans that guitarist and RCA Victor Records executive Chet Akins drew up on a paper napkin. Over 47,000 songs were recorded here in the humble RCA Studio B, including "Oh Lonesome Me" (Don Gibson), "Only Daddy That'll Walk the Line" (Waylon Jennings), "I Will Always Love You" (Dolly Parton), "Only the Lonely" (Roy Orbison), "All I Have to Do Is Dream" (Everly Brothers), "Kiss an Angel Good Morning" (Charlie Pride), and "Are You Lonesome Tonight?" (Elvis Presley).

Audio engineer Bill Porter added two- by four-foot fiberglass acoustic ceiling panels, the "Porter Pyramids," and used the "latest innovations in sound equipment," according to a 1957 *Tennessean* article, to capture the smooth tempos, sophisticated background vocals, and crooning lead vocals that would characterize the Nashville sound. Porter used tape to mark an X on the linoleum-tiled floor, the so-called "sweet spot," where the stars knew they'd find the perfect acoustics to record their next hit. RCA Studio B was a big part of the city's identity as a recording center, centering what would become "Music Row," the heart of Nashville's music industry.

"The sound here just seems to hug you," said country singer Connie Smith, who recorded her first single, chart-topper "Once a Day," at Studio B in 1964. "The musicians were all close, and we could communicate with our eyes. When I'd sing, my voice would go out, and I could tell what was happening by how it hit the walls. I could control what I was doing; other studios are so big that it disappears."

The studio closed on August 17, 1977, the day after Elvis Presley died, and ownership was transferred to the Country Music Hall of Fame and Museum in 1992. The historic site remains a semi-working recording studio, but the museum hosts guided tours during the day.

Don't forget to take a look at the building's unassuming exterior: Dolly Parton, in her 1994 memoir, *My Life and Other Unfinished Business*, recounted how she was rushing to her first recording session at Studio B in October 1967 when she accidentally drove her car through the side wall of the building: "In my rush to get to the studio that day, I forgot one basic element of driving—braking. I arrived at the old RCA studio on Music Row and plowed right into the side of the building. Bricks were still falling onto the hood of my car as I walked nonchalantly into the recording session as if nothing had happened. When we took a break a little later, the men went outside to have a cigarette and noticed my car

> To me, **SONGWRITING IS THE BACKBONE OF NASHVILLE.** Looks can go, fads can go, **BUT A GOOD SONG LASTS FOREVER.**
>
> ALAN JACKSON

stuck in the wall. They commented on it, but I never did say anything or confess that it was my car. That old studio is now a historic site in Nashville. If you visit there, you can still see where the bricks are slightly different in that particular spot. The way Chet Atkins reacted, I think he knew whose car it was; Chet, if you did, I thank you for never letting on."

1611 Roy Acuff Place, Nashville; countrymusichalloffame.org /experiences/studio-b

♪ BLUEBIRD CAFE
IN THE ROUND

NASHVILLE, THE "SONGWRITING CAPITAL OF THE WORLD," is a place where musicians from around the world gather to share their passion for lyrics. "It's basically a city of songwriters, and that's what gives it its strength, that's what gives it its lasting ability," summed up singer, songwriter, and musician Emmylou Harris. "You've got people making all different kinds of music, and that's what attracts me to Nashville as Music City."

The Bluebird Cafe is Nashville's star-making listening room. The unassuming venue in a strip mall on the outskirts of the city is where Music City songwriters and artists go to debut new material. Some songwriters wind up scoring record deals on the spot. Singer-songwriter Taylor Swift

> People think my life has been tough, but I think **IT HAS BEEN A WONDERFUL JOURNEY.** The older you get, the more you realize **IT'S NOT WHAT HAPPENS, BUT HOW YOU DEAL WITH IT.**
> TINA TURNER

was discovered at the Bluebird Cafe by music executive Scott Borchetta when she was just fourteen.

Artists and songwriters, both rising stars and established icons, are invited to perform in the intimate "In the Round" showcase, a concept created in Nashville: Four songwriters are seated in the center of the listening room, where they take turns playing their songs and accompanying one other, both instrumentally and with harmony vocals.

Reservations are recommended as seating is limited, though you can also wait in line—arrive early!—and keep your fingers crossed that a seat opens up at the last minute.

4104 Hillsboro Pike, Nashville; bluebirdcafe.com

♪ TINA TURNER'S SCHOOLHOUSE AND THE HOME OF "SLEEPY" JOHN ADAM ESTES
WEST TENNESSEE DELTA HERITAGE CENTER

VISITORS ARE INVITED TO STEP INSIDE SITES that inspired local legends—Tina Turner's childhood schoolhouse and the last home of blues

pioneer "Sleepy" John Estes—just off the Music Highway (Interstate 40 at Exit 56), between Memphis and Nashville, in historic Brownsville, Tennessee, at the West Tennessee Delta Heritage Center.

Tina Turner was born Anna Mae Bullock on November 26, 1939, here in Brownsville. She attended first through eighth grade in this tiny schoolhouse, built by her great-uncle in 1889. Though she sang in her church choir as a child, it wasn't until she first saw Ike Turner perform with his band, the Kings of Rhythm, at the Manhattan Club in East St. Louis that she turned toward a musical career. One night, she grabbed the mic from Kings of Rhythm drummer Eugene Washington and belted out the B.B. King blues ballad, "You Know I Love You," and the rest is history. She joined Ike Turner's Kings of Rhythm in 1957, and in 1960, she debuted as Tina Turner with the hit duet single "A Fool in Love."

Turner went on to become one of the best-selling recording artists of all time, selling over 100 million records worldwide. Today, this one-room schoolhouse preserves the memorabilia of its most famous former student. Among the original school desks, Turner's glitzy costumes, gold records, and high school yearbook offer a glimpse into the childhood of the celebrated diva.

"There was only one teacher, and she taught four to five subjects," said Turner. "Reading, writing, and arithmetic. My favorite subject was reading and recess. My least favorite, arithmetic."

Brent Moore

Next door stands the home of country blues guitarist, songwriter, and vocalist "Sleepy" John Estes. Estes was born in nearby Ripley, Tennessee, in 1899 but grew up here in Brownsville. While working as a field hand as a teenager in the 1920s, Estes began to perform at local parties and picnics with his buddies, harmonica virtuoso Hammie Nixon and guitarist and mandolin player James "Yank" Rachell. Estes was known for his high-pitched "crying" vocal style and his lyrics that recall his hardscrabble life experiences ("Working Man Blues") and freight train hopping ("Special Agent [Railroad Police Blues]"),

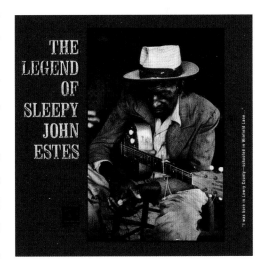

and the people he knew here in Brownsville, including a judge ("Lawyer Clark Blues"), an auto mechanic ("Vassie Williams' Blues"), and a ("Special Agent [Railroad Police Blues]").

Estes lived in this two-room shotgun-style home with his wife and seven kids. Shotgun homes were the most popular style of house in the southern United States from the end of the American Civil War through the 1920s. Legend says they got their name because their simple design meant that a bullet shot through the front door could exit the back door without hitting anything.

Estes, who earned his nickname because of his unusual and useful ability to sleep standing up, famously said, "They called me sleepy, but I never missed a note."

121 Sunny Hill Cove, Brownsville, TN; westtnheritage.com

BILLY TRIPP'S MINDFIELD

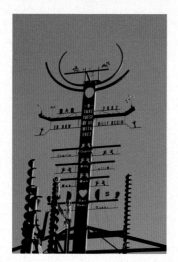

Outsider artist Bill Tripp has been gathering metal for over thirty years to create what is now billed as the tallest freestanding sculpture in Tennessee, "Billy Tripp's Mindfield." This maze of found metal, which grows year after year, details Tripp's life story and will only be complete, Tripp says, when he dies and is interred amid his vast, salvaged creation.

1 Mindfield Alley, Brownsville, TN; sites.google.com/site/billytripp /home

HELEN'S BBQ

Helen Turner is one of the few female pit cooks in the country. At her signature restaurant, Helen's BBQ, she cooks the most sublime BBQ pulled pork, smoked bologna, and Polish sausage you'll ever dig into on an open pit.

1016 N. Washington Ave., Brownsville, TN; facebook.com /pages/Helens-Bar-B-Q/114965458521552

Southern Foodways Alliance

MEMPHIS

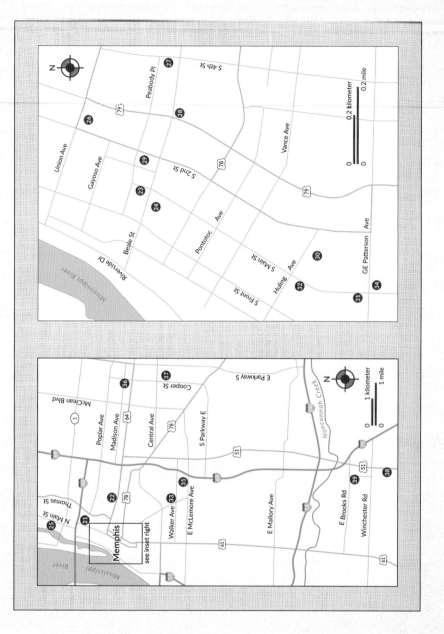

21. Lauderdale Courts Apartments

22. Sun Studio

23. Beale Street

24. Orpheum Theatre

25. Memphis Area Transit Authority (MATA) Vintage Trolley

26. Peabody Hotel Ducks

27. W.C. Handy House Museum

28. Memphis Rock 'n' Soul Museum

29. Memphis Music Hall of Fame

30. The Lorraine Motel–National Civil Rights Museum

31. Earnestine & Hazel's

32. Blues Hall of Fame Museum

33. The Four Way

34. Arcade Restaurant

35. Stax Museum of American Soul Music

36. Lafayette's Music Room

37. Memphis Gong Chamber

38. Graceland

39. Tigerman Karate Dojo and Museum

> "People who come to Memphis notice cultural collisions. Other cities may have similar black and white populations that interact or segregate themselves exactly as Memphis does, but something about this city tunes our antennae to such things. Whether knowing its history we project it, or we are drawn to it by forces we cannot see; race relations, also known as music, is the lifeblood of Memphis. The first song to top the pop, country, and rhythm 'n' blues charts came from Memphis . . . Carl Perkins' 'Blue Suede Shoes.' **MEMPHIS MUSIC IS A CONCEPT, NOT A SOUND.**
>
> ROBERT GORDON, *IT CAME FROM MEMPHIS*

♪ LAUDERDALE COURTS APARTMENTS
THE HOME THAT SET THE STAGE FOR ELVIS

THE RED-BRICK LAUDERDALE COURTS APARTMENT COMPLEX was one of America's first public housing projects. The 449 apartment units, designed to promote "a sense of community," housed families searching for a better life. Beginning in September 1949, those families included Vernon and Gladys Love Presley and their thirteen-year-old son Elvis. The humble apartment was a step up from their former two-room shotgun house in Tupelo, Mississippi, and the move to Memphis would put young Elvis steps away from music clubs on Beale Street.

When he first moved here, Elvis was shy and would practice singing and playing his guitar in the shared basement laundry room located directly under their apartment (just imagine his voice echoing among the washers and dryers!). It wasn't long before he started sneaking out his bedroom window overlooking Third Street to explore the city's music scene. He grew his sideburns and began slicking his hair with rose oil and Vaseline, and soon he was performing his first concerts in the communal courtyard.

Though he was nervous performing outside the Lauderdale Courts' courtyard, Elvis sang and played the guitar for a larger audience when he competed in a talent show at his school, L. C. Humes High School. "I wasn't popular in school . . . I failed at music—only thing I ever failed. And then they entered me in the talent show . . . when I came onstage, I heard people kind of rumbling and whispering and so forth, 'cause nobody knew I even sang. It was amazing how popular I became in school after that."

Elvis was still living here when he cut his first record, a two-sided acetate disc featuring "My Happiness" and "That's When Your Heartaches Begin," at Sam Phillips' Memphis Recording Service in January 1954.

In the mid-1990s, the Lauderdale Courts were slated for demolition until a local developer, preservationists, and Elvis fans stepped in to save them. Today, Lauderdale Courts is listed on the National Register of Historic Places, though they've been renovated into hip new apartments and have a new name (Uptown Square).

The Presley family apartment has been carefully restored to replicate the period style during their residency, and you can take a tour (seasonally) or spend the night in Elvis' teenage home. As you settle off to sleep in Elvis' bedroom, it's easy to imagine him sitting in the window, playing his guitar in the wee hours of the night, his future still but a dream.

252 N. Lauderdale St., Memphis; (901) 523-8662; facebook.com /lauderdalecourts/

♪ SUN STUDIO
BIRTHPLACE OF ROCK 'N ROLL

WREC RADIO ENGINEER SAM PHILLIPS always dreamed of opening his own recording studio. In January 1950, he opened the doors to the studio that would change the course of American music history, Memphis Recording Service, at 706 Union Ave. with his assistant and longtime friend, Marion Keisker. With the motto, "We Record Anything, Anywhere, Anytime," Phillips' open-door policy allowed anyone to stroll in and record a single.

One fellow who strolled in to record a single was eighteen-year-old Elvis Presley, who paid for a few minutes to record "My Happiness" and "That's When Your Heartaches Begin" onto a two-sided disc he intended to gift to his mother. However, he also hoped he might be discovered here at the studio that became known for nurturing new talent. When Marion Keisker asked what kind of singer he was, he replied, "I sing all kinds . . . I don't sound like nobody." Keisker jotted in her notebook: "Good ballad singer. Hold."

Presley cut a second acetate in January 1954. Still, it wasn't until he returned in July that Elvis found his footing as a recording artist when, in the wee hours of the night, just as he was about to give up and go home, he belted out a blues number, Arthur Crudup's "That's All Right." Elvis was accompanied by guitarist Winfield "Scotty" Moore, who recalled, "All of a sudden, Elvis just started singing this song, jumping around and acting the fool, and then Bill picked up his bass, and he started acting the fool, too, and I started playing with them. Sam, I think, had the door to the control booth open . . . he stuck his head out and said, 'What are you doing?' And we said, 'We don't know.' 'Well, back up,' he said, 'try to find a place to start, and do it again.'" Three days later, the song was picked up and played by popular Memphis DJ Dewey Phillips, and listeners began calling in and asking for more.

A few years earlier—on March 5, 1951—"Rocket 88," which some consider to be the first rock 'n roll single, was recorded here. Jackie Brenston and his Delta Cats (Ike Turner's Kings of Rhythm backup band) recorded the raucous "Rocket 88"—a hit song born of a minor accident: When the guitarist's amp speaker cone broke, the band improvised by stuffing the broken cone with newspapers. The result was a distorted, unbridled sound that intrigued Phillips so much that he amplified it during recording.

"I think that 'Rocket 88' is R&B, but I think 'Rocket 88' is the cause of rock and roll existing," Ike Turner explained in an interview with record producer Holger Petersen. "Sam Phillips got Dewey Phillips to play 'Rocket 88' on his program—and this is like the first black record to be played on a white radio station—and, man, all the white kids broke out to the record shops to buy it. So that's when Sam Phillips got the idea, 'Well, man, if I get me a white boy to sound like a black boy, then I got me a gold mine,' which is the truth. So, that's when he got Elvis, and he got Jerry Lee Lewis and a bunch of other guys, and so they named it rock and roll rather than R&B, and so this is the reason I think rock and roll exists—not that 'Rocket 88' was the first one, but that was what caused the first one."

So many legends came to Sun Studio to record and release their early records—Howlin' Wolf, Junior Parker, James Cotton, B.B. King, and Johnny Cash. Jerry Lee Lewis, Carl Perkins, and Roy Orbison. The Million Dollar Quartet was born here on December 4, 1956, when Elvis, Jerry Lee Lewis, Johnny Cash, and Carl Perkins popped in for an impromptu jam session.

After hours, Sun Studio is still a working recording studio; during the day, visitors are invited to tour the tiny studio where so much music history was made.

"Music is not an option, really, with people," Phillips told National Public Radio host Terry Gross in a 1997 interview. "We take it for

granted—people that are in it professionally and people that just love it to listen to and people that can take it or leave it. But music is the single most important element outside of—I guess we need a little oxygen to breathe in order to be able to listen to music. But there is nothing on the face of God's Earth that gives us more solace in more different areas, in more different ways than music."

David Jones

CHESS RECORDS

CHESS RECORDS, founded in Chicago by brothers Phil and Leonard Chess, both Jewish immigrants from Poland, in 1950 recorded some of the most beloved LPs in music history. In addition to bringing the blues of Muddy Waters, Etta James, Chuck Berry, Bo Diddley, John Lee Hooker, and Howlin' Wolf to the world's attention, the label shaped the future of American-born music by inspiring and recording songs by rock 'n roll artists, including The Rolling Stones, who recorded "2120 South Michigan Avenue," a song named after Chess Records' address, here in June 1964. Today Chess Records is home to the Blues Heaven Foundation, which offers behind-the-scenes studio tours and concerts in the adjacent garden.

2120 S. Michigan Ave., Chicago, IL, bluesheaven.com

♪ BEALE STREET
THE COOLEST STREET IN THE NATION

BEALE STREET IS ONE OF THE most beloved, bustling streets in America. Its three blocks of nightclubs, restaurants, and shops sway to the beat of a melting pot of music. On any given night, you might hear blues, jazz, rock 'n roll, R&B, and gospel streaming through the air. Once upon a time, musical legends sang their hearts out onstage here, and yet you still might catch a rising star today on the coolest street in the USA.

Beale Street, which runs from the mighty Mississippi River to East Street, was created in 1841 when entrepreneur and developer Colonel

Robertson Topp purchased a tract of land, developed a thoroughfare, and named it Beale Avenue, after a hero of the Mexican-American War. Soon the street was lined with shops that sold wares unloaded from ships that docked on the Mississippi River at the street's end. By the 1860s, Black traveling musicians began performing to the impromptu audience formed by merchants and shoppers on the bustling street.

By the 1870s, when Memphis suffered a series of devastating yellow fever outbreaks, the city was forced to forfeit its charter in 1879. With property devalued, another entrepreneur stepped in: American Robert Church, who believed Memphis would rise again after the crippling pandemics. His move would make him the first African American millionaire in the South.

In 1890, the first formal music venue, the Grand Opera House, later known as the Orpheum Theatre, rose on the corner of Beale Street and Main Street. Beale Street Baptist Church, the oldest surviving African American church in Tennessee, laid its cornerstone in 1869 and would rise to play a key role in the early Civil Rights movement in Memphis (the church also housed the office of Ida B. Wells, a civil rights–focused journalist and the editor of *Free Speech*, an anti-segregationist paper). And in 1899, Church invested in the city once again when he established Church Park at the corner of Fourth and Beale: Blues musicians gathered at the park and played at the park's auditorium, which could seat two thousand people. In 1909, a trumpet player by the name of W. C. Handy moved from Alabama to Beale Avenue, where he served as a music teacher for the Knights of Pythias Band. Handy's 1916 song "Beale Street Blues" was the impetus for changing the street's name from Beale Avenue to Beale Street.

By the early 1900s, Beale Street was hopping with revelers who frequented its many nightclubs owned by African Americans. The street peaked from the 1920s to the 1940s, when musicians gravitated to the street's musical vibe and created a subgenre of blues known as Memphis blues.

When W. C. Handy, the "Father of the Blues," published "The Memphis Blues" in 1909, it was the first blues song to be written down and the first song to encapsulate the spirit of the street.

Folks, I've just been down, down to Memphis town,
That's where the people smile, smile on you all the while.
Hospitality, they were good to me.
I couldn't spend a dime and had the grandest time.
I went out a dancing with a Tennessee dear,
They had a fellow there named Handy with a band you
should hear
And while the folks gently swayed, all the band folks
played real harmony.
I never will forget the tune that Handy called the Memphis Blues.
Oh yes, them Blues.

Beale Street still glows with neon, music still spills out of its nightclubs, and jam sessions still extend into the wee hours of the night. The street also hosts the Beale Street Music Festival, which brings headliners from various musical genres to Tom Lee Park at the end of Beale Street on the Mississippi River, kicking off the citywide Memphis in May Festival.

♪ ORPHEUM THEATRE
"THE SOUTH'S FINEST THEATRE"

SO MUCH OF THE HISTORY of entertainment in America has unfolded here on the corner of Main and Beale Streets. After a series of yellow fever epidemics nearly took Memphis off the map, the Grand Opera

House rose from the devastation in 1890. Billed "The South's Finest Theatre," the grand theater hosted singers, musicians, and magicians performing their way across the country along the Orpheum Circuit (hence the 1907 name change to the Orpheum Theatre). Singer Blossom Seeley, the "Queen of Syncopation" who helped carry jazz and ragtime into mainstream American

MEMPHIS AREA TRANSIT AUTHORITY VINTAGE TROLLEY

The most nostalgic way to get around downtown Memphis is by trolley car. The Memphis Area Transit Authority (MATA) recently restored the vintage trolley passenger operations to the Main Street Trolley rail line, and three lines operate daily, making stops near downtown historic sites, including Beale Street. Base trolley fares cost just $1 per ride, and daily passes can be purchased for $2. Be on the lookout for Mary, one of the Orpheum's most spirited patrons: Legend states that she was injured in a 1928 trolley accident and carried into the theater, where she passed away. Some believe her ghost still lingers among the audience.

matatransit.com

PEABODY HOTEL DUCKS

MAKE WAY FOR DUCKLINGS

Beloved for its charm and Southern hospitality, the Peabody Memphis, also known as the "South's Grand Hotel," has been welcoming guests since 1869. But the grand hotel is perhaps best known for its five resident mallard ducks, which march daily through the lobby at 11 a.m. and 5 p.m.

When and how did this beloved party of ducks check into the hotel?

Sometime in the 1930s, general manager Frank Shutt and his buddy Chip Barwick returned from a weekend hunting trip to Arkansas and let their live duck decoys swim for a spell in the lobby fountain. The three small English call ducks—Peabody, Gayoso, and Chisca—were so well received that the tradition lives on over ninety years later.

Five North American mallards live in the hotel's rooftop "Royal Duck Palace," a tiny replica of the hotel featuring its very own fountain of a bronze duck spitting water. Raised by a local farmer and a friend of the hotel, each team of ducks lives at the hotel for only three months before retiring to the farm to live the wild duck life.

The Peabody is rich in music history, too: The studios of Memphis radio station WREC were located in the hotel's basement for over forty years, and the hotel's restaurant, the Skyway, was a popular nightspot, especially during the Big Band era when CBS broadcast a weekly radio program direct from its stage.

In 1931, jazz great Louis Armstrong and his band were arrested in Memphis and forced to spend a night in jail after Armstrong sat beside a White woman (his manager's wife) on a bus. The following day, Armstrong and his all-Black band played for an all-White audience at the Peabody Hotel, opening with a song Armstrong dedicated to the Memphis Police Department, "I'll Be Glad When You're Dead You Rascal You."

149 Union Ave., Memphis; peabodymemphis.com

music, performed here on October 16, 1923. Just as the last patrons left the theater that fateful night, a mysterious fire broke out that destroyed the building.

But that wasn't the end. Renowned architects C. W. and George L. Rapp designed the "New Orpheum," a 2,800-seat gilded theater with crystal chandeliers and a 1,100-pipe Mighty Wurlitzer organ. In the early days, vaudeville and musical acts—including Louis Armstrong, Duke Ellington, and the Folies Bergere—graced this stage. Then came a new entertainment craze: silent movies. And then the "talkies." Decades of films.

By 1982, the ornate theater was showing some wear and tear and underwent a $5 million restoration to its 1928 opulence. It was one of the first buildings in Memphis to be added to the National Register of Historic Places.

To experience "The South's Finest Theatre," settle in for a Broadway show (since 1977, the Orpheum has served as the Mid-South home of touring Broadway productions), a performance by Ballet Memphis, or a concert, comedy show, movie, or festival. The theater hosts a performance almost every day of the week, maintaining its mission to "entertain, educate and enlighten" through the performing arts.

203 S. Main St., Memphis; orpheum-memphis.com

W.C. HANDY HOUSE MUSEUM
HOME OF THE "FATHER OF THE BLUES"

W.C. HANDY, THE "FATHER OF THE BLUES," stands as one of America's most influential songwriters ever. When he moved to Memphis in 1909 from Alabama, he settled into this two-room shotgun home on Jeanette Place in South Memphis. The turn-of-the-century home was restored in the 1980s and today sits on Beale Street in downtown Memphis, where

it displays photos and memorabilia that offer insight into the life of the first composer to publish music in the blues genre.

He was born William Christopher Handy in a log cabin in Florence, Alabama, on November 16, 1873. Handy saved up money to buy his first guitar—secretly, because his father, a Methodist pastor, believed that musical instruments were the "tools of the devil." When his father saw the musical tool, he ordered him to return it and arranged for his son to take lessons for a slightly holier musical instrument, the organ. Handy instead learned to play the cornet and joined a local band, a secret he kept from his parents.

At first, his musical career took a backseat to teaching. Once he realized he could make more money working at a factory, he moved to Bessemer, Alabama, to work at a pipe works plant. In his spare time, he organized a small string orchestra.

In the early 1900s, Handy traveled throughout Mississippi and soaked in the popular music of the Delta. Later, he would incorporate elements of this Black folk music into his own musical style.

Thomas R. Machnitzki

In 1909, Handy moved into this home in Memphis and began playing the clubs on Beale Street with his band. The tiny home's most prized artifact on display is the desk at which W.C. Handy wrote many of his most famous songs, including "The Memphis Blues," the first published blues composition.

Less than 500 feet from his former home stands a life-size statue of W.C. Handy (200 Beale St.). Leone Tommassi sculpted the bronze statue at the Fuse Marinelli foundry in Florence, Italy. It was placed here at the entrance to the park in 1960. A commemorative plaque on the monument reads: "In memory of W. C. Handy, Composer, Music Publisher, Father of the Blues."

352 Beale St., Memphis; wchandymemphis.org

♪ MEMPHIS ROCK 'N' SOUL MUSEUM
MUSIC FEEDS THE SOUL

MEMPHIS IS A MUSE FOR MUSIC. From blues and soul to rock and hip hop, so many musical artists have been born or raised in Bluff City.

King Curtis' hit song "Memphis Soul Stew" shares the secret recipe behind the city's musical soul:

Today's special is "Memphis Soul Stew"
We sell so much of this
People wonder what we put in it
We gon' tell you right now

Gimme about a half a teacup of bass
Now, I need a pound of fatback drums
Now, give me four tablespoons of boiling Memphis guitars
This goin' taste all right

Now, just a little pinch of organ
Now, give me a half a pint of horns
Place on the burner and bring to a boil
That's it, that's it, that's it, right there.

The Memphis Rock 'n' Soul Museum shines a spotlight on the Memphis musical legends that rose to the top despite racial and socio-economic obstacles.

"Memphis music is grittier than Motown," said singer and songwriter Isaac Hayes, one of the creative forces behind the Southern soul music label Stax Records. "It's closer to where blues began. It's down-home soul music born out of blues and gospel. All over the world, Memphis soul music has been revered and recognized."

The highlight here is the museum's MP3 audio guide, which will guide you through the various exhibits and play over 100 songs recorded in and around Memphis from the 1930s through the 1970s.

On display are more than thirty instruments that played

H. Michael Miley

the hit songs and forty costumes worn by the legends that sang them. You can see the piano on which Ike Turner wrote "Rocket 88"; the Isana guitar that Elvis bought while serving in the armed forces in Germany and used to serenade Priscilla; and the microphone on which Carl Perkins first recorded "Blue Suede Shoes." There's even Hayes' diamond and emerald wristwatch; the face of the watch is a three-dimensional grand piano that must be raised to see the dial.

191 Beale St., Memphis; memphisrocknsoul.org

♪ MEMPHIS MUSIC HALL OF FAME
HONORING MEMPHIS' LEGENDARY MUSICIANS

MEMPHIS' MOST ICONIC MUSICIANS are honored here, with interactive exhibits, video interviews, and memorabilia. Items on display include Jerry Lee Lewis' customized Cadillac, which includes his monogram on the leather Landau Roof, and a custom Rolls Royce grill; Elvis Presley's original briefcase "mobile telephone" from the era when smartphones were only a dream; "The Tennessee Kids" bandstand (and Nike sneakers) from Justin Timberlake's 20/20 Experience World Tour; and the Oscar presented by the Academy Awards to Three 6 Mafia, the first rap group to win "Best Original Score" award for "It's Hard Out Here for a Pimp" from the 2005 film *Hustle & Flow*.

The Memphis Music Hall of Fame, established in 2012 and administered by the Memphis Rock 'n' Soul Museum, is by the former location of Lansky Brothers' Clothier. The clothier once dressed many of the inductees, including Elvis Presley, Jerry Lee Lewis, Edward Lee Floyd, Rufus Thomas, Count Basie, Lionel Hampton, Duke Ellington, and B.B. King.

126 S. 2nd St., Memphis; memphismusichalloffame.com

THE LORRAINE MOTEL—
NATIONAL CIVIL RIGHTS MUSEUM

FREEDOM CAN'T WAIT

In 1945, entrepreneur Walter Bailey purchased the Marquette Hotel at Mulberry Street and Huling Avenue and renamed it for his wife Loree and the song "Sweet Lorraine." Listed in the Negro Motorist Green Book, a travel guide highlighting businesses that would accept Black customers during segregation, the Lorraine Motel was an upscale, safe haven for Black travelers. Many of its guests, including Ray Charles, Aretha Franklin, Lionel Hampton, and Ethel Waters, were in Memphis to record at local studios.

But the motel is perhaps best remembered for the tragedy that took place on the balcony just outside room 306. The Rev. Dr. Martin Luther King Jr. was assassinated here on April 4, 1968.

Today the former motel houses the National Civil Rights Museum, where interactive exhibits tell the story of the fight for civil rights, from the beginning of the resistance during slavery to the present day.

Visitors can still peer into room 306, which was never rented again. A true time capsule, the room is still outfitted with its rotary telephone, old-school television, and

midcentury modern decor. A white wreath hangs on the balcony in remembrance.

On Dr. King's birth and death dates, January 15 and April 4, the museum honors his legacy through a series of events with prominent civil rights leaders and scholars while local musicians perform in front of the balcony where King was assassinated.

The MLK Soul Concert Series invites music lovers to park their lawn chairs on the motel's lawn on Friday evenings in September for free concerts with music ranging from jazz to soul.

450 Mulberry St., Memphis; civilrightsmuseum.org

> ## Our lives begin to end the day
> # WE BECOME SILENT ABOUT THINGS THAT MATTER.
> ### DR. MARTIN LUTHER KING, JR.

♪ EARNESTINE & HAZEL'S
MOST SPIRITED DIVE BAR IN MEMPHIS

EARNESTINE AND HAZEL'S is the most beloved dive bar in Nashville, a place where you can bite into the signature "soul burger," dance into the wee hours of the night to soul, jazz, and blues, and even mingle with a spirited jukebox.

In the 1930s, this late nineteenth-century building housed a pharmacy owned by Abe Plough. At age sixteen, he whipped up "Plough's Antiseptic Healing Oil," a "sure cure for any ill of man or beast." When it became the hottest miracle med, Plough branched out into cosmetics. He added aspirin to his line of suspect cure-alls in 1920, buying the St. Joseph Company outright, a step he called his "first on the road to the big time." When he moved his operations into a $2 million factory on East Jackson Avenue, Plough gifted the entire building to Earnestine and Hazel, two hair stylists (and cousins) that lived in an apartment on the top floor.

Earnestine and Hazel were business-minded too, and they turned the building into a cafe. Earnestine's husband, Sunbeam, worked as a talent booking agent at a nearby nightclub, Club Paradise. After wrapping up their gigs at Club Paradise, legends the likes of Muddy Waters, Tina Turner, Aretha Franklin, Ray Charles, Bo Diddley, Sam Cook, Chuck Berry, and Jackie Wilson went on over to Earnestine and Hazel's, where they knew they could always find a home-cooked meal, good booze, great music, and a little hanky panky (Earnestine and Hazel ran another more lucrative side gig, renting out the eight rooms on the top floor to local prostitutes).

Then came the economic downturn of the 1970s. When Club Paradise closed, so did Earnestine and Hazel's.

Fast forward to 1992, and Earnestine and Hazel's was restored to its former glory as Memphis' hottest after-hours hangout spot.

The Unearthed Memphis podcast reports that Earnestine and Hazel's is one of the most haunted spots in town: "At least thirteen people died in the building. . . . It's been reported that you get a feeling of sadness when you go upstairs and a feeling of relief, like a weight has been lifted when you go back downstairs. People have also said they've felt hands touching them when they go upstairs. I bet that's the spirits of the ladies who used to work there, trying to beckon you to a room." In addition to paranormal investigations documenting poltergeist activity, the jukebox here is also known to burst into a song suddenly and has excellent taste in music. Once, when a paranormal researcher was visiting, a bartender claimed the machine started playing "Sympathy for the Devil" on its own. And on the day James Brown died, the jukebox blasted out "I Feel Good," unprompted.

531 S. Main St., Memphis; earnestineandhazel.com

Sean Davis

BLUES HALL OF FAME MUSEUM
HONORING THOSE WHO MADE THE BLUES SO TIMELESS

THE BLUES HALL OF FAME, started in 1980 by the Memphis-born Blues Foundation, honors those who have made their indelible mark on the blues. An anonymous committee of blues scholars representing all subsets of blues music nominates new members every spring, and the Blues Hall of Fame Induction ceremony is held annually on the evening before *The Blues Music Awards*.

The Blues Hall of Fame Museum, which opened in 2015, has ten galleries honoring 400 inductees through precious artifacts, photographs, and recordings of their music and words of wisdom. The upstairs Legendary Rhythm and Blues Cruise gallery hosts traveling exhibits that rotate every four months. Permanent collection highlights include Pee Wee Crayton's Fender Stratocaster guitar, Donald "Duck" Dunn's Lakland electric bass, Matt "Guitar" Murphy's McHugh guitar, a dress worn by

John Phelan

"THE BLUES TELLS A STORY.
Every line of the blues has a meaning.
JOHN LEE HOOKER

Bettye LaVette when she performed at the Kennedy Center, and Stevie Ray Vaughan's kimono.

One of the Blues Foundation's most significant achievements is the Handy Artists Relief Trust (HART) Fund, which helps blues musicians and their families in need by providing medical and dental care and funeral and burial expenses.

The Blues Foundation also hosts the International Blues Challenge, an annual event that invites blues societies from around the world to send their best band and solo/duo performers for a head-to-head challenge along Beale Street (blues.org/international-blues-challenge).

421 S. Main St., Memphis; blues.org/hall-of-fame-museum/

THE FOUR WAY
FOOD FOR THE SOUL

NOT MUCH HAS CHANGED at the Four Way in the past three-quarters of a century: The menu at this oldest soul food restaurant in Memphis offers only food classics like neckbones and fried catfish, and the vegetables—boiled okra, fried green tomatoes, turnip greens—are still all prepped fresh daily in the kitchen. The desserts—strawberry cake, lemon meringue pie, peach cobbler—are still to die for. It's one of the few places in town where you can enjoy a full Thanksgiving dinner any given day of the week. You can still expect a warm welcome from behind the counter

and a dining room filled with people digging into food that fills both the belly and the soul.

Beyond a slice of the best sweet potato pie in town, the Four Way also serves up a slice of Memphis history.

Located at the intersection of Walker Avenue and Mississippi Boulevard, the restaurant has long been a community gathering place where people break bread together. Framed photographs of frequent guests the likes of Dr. Martin Luther King Jr., Aretha Franklin, and Rosa Parks line the walls.

When founders Irene and Clint Cleaves opened the Four Way in 1946, it was attached to a pool hall and barber shop. It quickly earned a

reputation for excellent food— food so delicious that it drew the community together and became one of the first naturally integrated restaurants in Memphis.

Clint Cleaves was the personal chauffeur of Memphis mayor E. H. Crump, and the diner has long been an unofficial meeting spot for local politicians. Civil rights leaders strategized over smothered pork chops, country-fried steak, and salmon croquettes. Music artists, including the two kings, Elvis and B.B. King, recorded their latest hits at nearby Stax Records and then strolled in to celebrate with a meat and three.

"So in a segregated time, this place was never segregated," current owner Patrice Thompson told Memphis Action News 5 in 2019. "And that was because of the warm arms of Mrs. Cleaves and Mr. Cleaves and the help of Mayor Crump. It meant a lot for them to be able to sit and have fine dining."

You also might recognize the Four Way from Drake's video for his hit single "Worst Behavior," co-directed by Drake himself. Dennis Graham, Drake's father, grew up in Memphis, and Drake often spent his summers here. The video features half of Drake's family tree, including his mustachioed dad and suited-up uncles, who open the video, standing outside his grandmother's house.

998 Mississippi Blvd., Memphis; fourway901.com

ARCADE RESTAURANT

Founded in 1919, the Arcade is Memphis' oldest restaurant and still maintains its classic midcentury modern decor. Try to sit at the Elvis booth toward the back of the restaurant (it was the King's favorite) and dig into a chocolate mudslide or sweet potato pancakes.

540 S. Main St., Memphis; arcaderestaurant.com

♪ STAX MUSEUM OF AMERICAN SOUL MUSIC
HOP ABOARD THE SOUL TRAIN

JAMES FRANK STEWART WORKED at a bank by day and played the fiddle by night for a local country music group, the Canyon Cowboys. Though he had an inkling he couldn't exactly swing a career as a professional musician, he set his sights on the next best job in the music biz: producer. Despite having zero experience or knowledge of the recording industry, he launched Satellite Records from a garage in 1957 when he cut his label's first record, "Blue Roses." Stewart recalled, "We didn't have any sound equipment or anything else but a small building and a lot of desire."

Unhappy with the low quality of his first production but still determined to make it big in the music biz, Stewart asked his music-loving sister Estelle Axton to join forces. They renamed their company Stax, a combination of the first two letters of their last names, Stewart and Axton. Axton took out a second mortgage on her home to invest in the business, purchased an Ampex 350 console recorder, and financed the move here in the former Capitol Theatre.

With limited funding for their new endeavor, the transformation of the theater was a DIY project for the sibling duo. The main theater was partitioned, and the control room was placed where the screen had once flickered with movies. The slanted main theater floor helped deaden the sound, creating a unique acoustical effect, a heavy, bassy sound that would ultimately become a critical factor in the signature Stax sound.

Peter Burke

In the summer of 1960, rhythm and blues, funk, soul, and blues artist Rufus Thomas and his daughter Carla recorded "Cause I Love You," the first recording at Stax. The song started as a regional hit, was picked up for national distribution by Atlantic Records, and eventually sold forty thousand copies.

The label went on to score several hits on the Billboard Hot 100 pop music chart. According to ethnomusicologist Rob Bowman, the label's use of "one studio, one equipment setup, the same set of musicians and a small group of songwriters led to a readily identifiable sound. It was a sound based on Black gospel, blues, country, and earlier forms of R&B. It became known as southern soul music."

Stax's biggest star—Otis Redding—arrived as a driver for Johnny Jenkins and the Pinetoppers, who had come to the studio to record an instrumental following the massive success of "Green Onions." Redding was allowed to sing after Jenkins' session had gone poorly, and the room fell silent. Redding would move to become the "King of Soul." *Rolling Stone* ranked Redding as number 21 on its list of the "100 Greatest Artists of All Time" and eighth on the list of the "100 Greatest Singers of All Time."

Today, the theater that became a recording studio is a museum that preserves the Stax story.

The music-centered museum welcomes guests with a re-creation of the true birthplace of soul music—a circa 1906 Mississippi Delta church that was carefully reassembled here. Studio A, where Stax artists recorded, has also been reassembled, down to the period recording equipment and the slanting floor that created Stax's unique sound. The walls in the museum's "Hall of Records" are lined with all the albums and singles released by Stax from 1957 to 1975, and you can listen to them all at the dedicated listening station.

The glittering gem of the museum is Isaac Hayes' custom Cadillac Eldorado with its 24-carat gold exterior trim. Purchased after he renegotiated a deal with Stax in 1972, the car boasts luxe amenities, including a refrigerated mini-bar, television, and white fur carpeting on the floorboards.

The Stax Museum of American Soul Music is also perhaps the only museum in the world with its own dance floor. "We understand it's hard not to dance when you listen to Stax tracks," the museum warns. "While most museums don't encourage dancing in the aisles, we invite you to shake what your mama gave you on the Express Yourself dance floor. Don't

> **Being in Kiss in the very first year and touring around the United States, WE FELT LIKE WE WERE TAKING OFF.** It was like somebody pushing you into the deep end of the pool, whether you can swim or not.
> —GENE SIMMONS

"When I was a child, ladies and gentlemen, I was a dreamer. I read comic books, and I was the hero of the comic book. I saw movies, and I was the hero in the movie. So every dream I ever dreamed has come true a hundred times . . . I learned very early in life that: 'Without a song, the day would never end; without a song, a man ain't got a friend; without a song, the road would never bend–without a song.' SO I KEEP SINGING A SONG. GOODNIGHT. THANK YOU.

ELVIS PRESLEY'S ACCEPTANCE SPEECH FOR A TEN OUT-STANDING YOUNG MEN OF THE NATION AWARD, 1970

TIGERMAN KARATE DOJO AND MUSEUM

Elvis trained at this working Karate Dojo, which is today managed by Joey Smith, Elvis' second cousin. The building looks just as it did in 1973 when the King received his black belt here under the guidance of his teacher, Kang Rhee. A mini museum features music and karate memorabilia as well as the ambulance that transported Elvis to Baptist Hospital on August 16, 1977, in an attempt to save his life.

3217 Lucibill Rd., Memphis; thetigermanmuseum.com

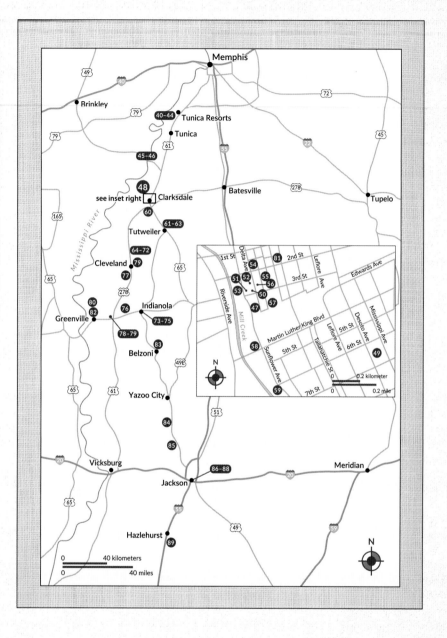

40. Gateway to the Blues Museum
41. Tunica Museum
42. Hollywood Cafe
43. Abbay & Leatherman
44. Blue and White Restaurant
45. Delta Dirt Distillery
46. *King Biscuit Time,* Live at the Delta Cultural Center
47. Muddy Water's Cabin at the Delta Blues Museum
48. Stovall Farms
49. WROX AM
50. Deak's Mississippi Saxophones & Blues Emporium
51. Meraki Roasting Company
52. Lunatic Fringe Luthiery
53. Quapaw Canoe Company
54. Hambone Gallery
55. Bluesberry Cafe
56. Cat Head Delta Blues & Folk Art
57. Ground Zero Blues Club
58. Red's
59. Riverside Hotel
60. Hopson Planting Company and the Shack Up Inn
61. W.C. Handy Encounters the Blues
62. Sonny Boy Williamson II's Gravesite
63. Emmett Till Interpretive Center/Tallahatchie County Courthouse
64. McCarty's Pottery
65. Po' Monkey's
66. Peter's Pottery
67. Mound Bayou
68. The Devil's Crossroads
69. Dockery Farms
70. Cast of Blues at Delta State University
71. Mississippi Delta Chinese Heritage Museum
72. Grammy Museum Mississippi
73. B.B. King Museum and Delta Interpretive Center
74. Indianola Pecan House
75. Club Ebony
76. Charley Patton's Gravesite
77. The Peavine Railroad
78. Leland Murals
79. The Birthplace of Kermit the Frog
80. Winterville Mounds
81. Yazoo Yaupon
82. Doe's Eat Place
83. Ethel Wright Mohamed Stitchery Museum
84. Blue Front Cafe
85. Mississippi Petrified Forest
86. Farish Street Historic District
87. Big Apple Inn
88. Hal & Mal's
89. Robert Johnson House

"THE MISSISSIPPI DELTA IS NOT ALWAYS DARK WITH RAIN.

Some autumn mornings, the sun rises over Moon Lake, or Eagle, or Choctaw, or Blue, or Roebuck, all the wide, deep waters of the state, and when it does, its dawn is as rosy with promise and hope as any other.

LEWIS NORDAN

♪ GATEWAY TO THE BLUES MUSEUM
WHERE THE BLUES BEGAN

THE GATEWAY TO THE BLUES MUSEUM greets motorists making their way down the Mississippi Blues Trail, a series of more than 200 interpretive markers that mark the sites that made the blues. It's just off the Blues Highway in Tunica, Mississippi.

The community is named after the indigenous peoples, the Tunica Indians, who thrived here before migrating south to the Lower Mississippi Valley. The Spanish conquistadors, under the command of Hernando de Soto, arrived here in 1541 in search of gold and settled the area after de Soto died of typhoid fever in 1542 (his body was "buried" in the Mississippi River). Later, the area developed an agricultural economy based on cotton, and by 1860, nearly 80 percent of the people here were enslaved.

The museum, housed in a circa 1895 train depot topped with a colorful neon sign welcoming visitors, has interactive exhibits that show how

the blending of cultures here—Native American, European, and African American—birthed the blues.

Almost all the most influential blues artists were born and raised in the Mississippi Delta, including B.B. King, Robert Johnson, Muddy Waters, Howlin' Wolf, Charley Patton, Son House, and Sonny Boy Williamson II.

Beyond the many artifacts and memorabilia on display, the highlight is the captivating "starlit" room encircled by Memphis-based artist George Hunt's striking paintings of eight blues legends. Also on display are W.C. Handy's first cornet and twenty guitars once owned by some of the greatest musical artists of all time. Interactive exhibits will teach you to play a lap steel guitar and a diddley bow. And at the in-museum recording studio, you can record your own blues song with provided background music (and it will be sent to you via email so you can share your latest hit with your friends and family).

13625 US-61, Tunica, MS; tunicatravel.com

♪ TUNICA MUSEUM
HAROLD "HARDFACE" CLANTON

TUNICA IS THE THIRD-LARGEST casino-gambling destination in the United States. Its many casinos are built on floating platforms in the Mississippi River to comply with state law.

Founded in 1997 and funded by local gambling revenues, the Tunica Museum highlights the history of Tunica County, beginning with an exhibit on the indigenous Tunica people and ending with an exhibit on the history of gambling in Tunica County.

One particular item on display recalls the era before gambling was legalized: the dice table owned by Tunica's first Black millionaire, Harold "Hardface" Clanton (1916–1982).

No one knows exactly if he was nicknamed for his effective, stone poker face or for sleeping with his face on the hard surface of craps tables. Still, Clanton, who specialized in a three-card poker game called Kotch, owned several businesses, including Harold's Cafe and "The Barn," an unofficial casino operation that would pave the way for legalizing gambling in 1991. Clanton hired renowned blues artists to play the music that kept the gambling booming, including B.B. King, Bobby Bland, Howlin' Wolf, Ike Turner, Albert King, Sonny Boy Williamson II, Robert Nighthawk, Frank Frost, and Houston Stackhouse. He also hired artists local to Tunica, including peg-legged Roosevelt "Barber" Parker, who along with his backup band the Silver Kings, once hosted a radio show on WDIA in Memphis.

1 Museum Blvd., Tunica, MS; tunicatravel.com

♪ HOLLYWOOD CAFE
STOP IN FOR THE FRIED DILL PICKLES, STAY FOR THE HISTORY

BACK WHEN THIS BUILD-ING HOUSED the commissary of the Frank Harbert plantation, bluesman Son House performed here accompanied by his guitarist Willie Brown or other legends of the local blues circle, including Robert  Johnson, Howlin' Wolf, Fiddlin' Joe Martin, Leroy Williams, Woodrow Adams, Willie Coffee, and Sol Henderson.

The Hollywood Cafe has been here since the summer of 1969 and is known for delectable fried pickles. Beyond that, Hollywood Cafe customers return again and again for the Mississippi catfish, hush puppies, fried shrimp platters, and steak.

Singer-songwriter Marc Cohn visited the cafe one day in 1985 to find Muriel Davis Wilkins, a retired schoolteacher, performing for the diners as she often did. Cohn joined her onstage. "The very last song we sang together that night was 'Amazing Grace,'" he remembered. "After we finished and people were applauding, Muriel leaned over and whispered in my ear: 'Child, you can let go now.' It was an incredibly maternal thing for her to say to me. Just like sitting in Reverend Al Green's church, I was again transformed. It was almost as if my mother was whispering in my ear. From the time I left Memphis and went back home to New York City, I knew I had a song in me about my experience there."

Cohn's hit song "Walking in Memphis" details his encounter with Wilkins in its lyrics:

Now Muriel plays piano

Every Friday at the Hollywood

And they brought me down to see her

And they asked me if I would

Do a little number

And I sang with all my might

She said,

"Tell me, are you a Christian child?"

And I said, "Ma'am, I am tonight."

1585 Old Commerce Rd., Robinsonville, MS; thehollywoodcafe.com

> "When Johnson started singing, he seemed like a guy WHO COULD HAVE SPRUNG FROM THE HEAD OF ZEUS IN FULL ARMOR. I immediately differentiated between him and anyone else I had ever heard.
> BOB DYLAN

♪ ABBAY & LEATHERMAN
TEENAGE HOME OF ROBERT JOHNSON

THE ABBAY & LEATHERMAN PLANTATION is one of the oldest and most extensive plantations in Mississippi. Though much of the land by the levee was sold or leased to casino developers—five casinos operate on what was once known as Commerce Landing—the plantation is still in operation today. Robert Johnson, the "King of the Blues," grew up here, living in a tenant shack by the levee with his family during the 1920s. Though many details of his life remain murky, and though he had little commercial success or recognition in his lifetime, performing primarily on street corners or at local parties and juke joints, it was here that Johnson dreamed up some of his most passionate songs.

The Indian Removal Act of 1828, the Treaty of Dancing Rabbit Creek in 1830, and the Treaty of Pontotoc in 1832 forced the area's native residents—Choctaws, Chickasaws, Cherokees, Seminoles, and Creeks—to give up their ancestral lands and relocate to reservations in the West. These same ancestral lands could then be bought from the state.

By 1841, Commerce Landing was booming; with a population of 5,000, it rivaled Memphis as a river trading center. A little over a decade earlier, twin brothers Richard and Anthony Abbay arrived at Commerce Landing from Nashville and bought former Native land at 50 cents an acre. Anthony ended up moving away, and Richard Abbay eventually partnered with his son-in-law, Samuel Richard Leatherman; thus the plantation was named the Abbay & Leatherman Plantation. When the

Civil War broke out, Richard Abbay had the foresight to sell his cotton for gold instead of Confederate money; he hid his earnings in a teapot, which he buried on the property. After the war, the farm continued to grow in acreage. More than 450 families lived and worked on the Abbey & Leatherman Plantation at its peak.

Sharecropping was the economic system that existed before the Civil War. Sharecroppers rented farmable land from plantation owners, who owned large patches of land, while also renting supplies and equipment from the farmer to grow cash crops, like tobacco and cotton. Though contracts varied, the sharecropper typically gave half of their harvest, or half of the money they made selling their harvest, to the landowner, in lieu of rent; any remaining proceeds were used to pay back the amount owing for the rented supplies and equipment, usually with interest. Though sharecroppers had the freedom to decide where, when, and how long they wanted to work, if the harvest was poor, many remained in debt until the next year and sometimes the next, making it almost impossible to earn enough income to buy their own piece of land to farm.

Robert Leroy Johnson, the illegitimate son of Julia Dodds and Noah Johnson, was born in Hazlehurst, Mississippi, on May 8, 1911. His mother was married to Charles Dodds, a landowner and furniture maker, and had ten children with him. When a lynch mob forced Charles Dodds to leave Hazlehurst after a dispute with White landowners, Julia brought baby Robert to live in Memphis with Charles. Robert Johnson spent his early childhood in Memphis before rejoining his mother around 1919 or 1920 after she married an illiterate sharecropper named Will "Dusty" Willis on the Abbay & Leatherman Plantation.

Johnson left the plantation around 1930 to pursue a career as an itinerant musician, reappearing two years later with such exceptional

BLUE AND WHITE RESTAURANT

Owned and operated for years by the Pure Oil Company, the Blue and White Cafe and Service Station opened in 1924 on Route 61 with a tobacco shop, newsstand, Greyhound bus stop, service station, and full-service restaurant service station under its chalet-style, bright blue rooftop. Stop in for gracious Southern hospitality and a smorgasbord of Southern favorites, including fluffy biscuits, fried green tomatoes, chicken livers and gravy, massive onion rings, deep-fried dill pickles, Mississippi catfish, and Southern fried chicken.

1355 US-61, Tunica, MS; blueandwhiterestaurant.com

DELTA DIRT DISTILLERY

(SWEET POTATO) SPIRIT OF THE MISSISSIPPI

Delta Dirt Distillery is a family-owned, small-batch distillery located in the "richest farmland in the country," Phillips County, in the heart of the Arkansas Delta.

The Williams family has deep roots in Arkansas, starting with "Papa" Joe Williams, the family patriarch. Papa Joe sharecropped the original 86 acres in the late 1800s; later, his son, U.D. Williams, farmed the same stretch of land. However, in 1949, U.D. bought the farm out of sharecropping, an incredible feat, even if it was with money earned from cotton and homemade corn-liquor moonshine.

The next generation to farm the land was Harvey Sr., who wisely diversified the operation and reinvented the farm for vegetable production, focusing on sweet potatoes and squash, which he shipped around the country. The distillery crafts its award-winning vodka with corn and sweet potatoes, so the vodka here is truly Delta-spirited.

Today the farm is in the hands of the family's fourth generation, and all of the produce and grains that make the coveted spirits are farmed locally. Delta Dirt Distillery is also the only Black farm distillery in the United States.

"Magic happens in the copper pot," distillery co-founder Harvey Williams told WREG Memphis in 2022. "I'm learning a lot more. . . . Hey, you guys are making yourselves proud, family proud, but you are making a lot of Black Americans proud!"

Stop by to shop the smooth spirits or book a behind-the-scenes tour to discover with your own eyes (and taste buds) how they transform sweet potatoes into premium vodka.

430 Cherry St., Helena, AR; deltadirtdistillery.com

guitar technique that Robinsonville blues luminary Son House remarked that Johnson must have "sold his soul to the devil."

The Abbay & Leatherman Plantation remains in the hands of the family today. A Mississippi Blue Trail marker is located just outside the plantation's former commissary.

1330 Leatherman Lane, Robinsonville, MS

KING BISCUIT TIME, LIVE AT THE DELTA CULTURAL CENTER
THE LONGEST-RUNNING BLUES RADIO SHOW IN THE WORLD

IN THE MID-1930s, when Helena, Arkansas, was still the terminal point on the former Missouri and North Arkansas Railroad that shuttled passengers and freight to Joplin, Missouri, the riverside town was considered "the Blues capital of the Delta." Among the musicians who regularly performed here at the halfway point between Memphis, Tennessee, and Vicksburg, Mississippi, were Robert Johnson, Johnny Shines, Sonny Boy Williamson II, Robert Nighthawk, Howlin' Wolf, Elmore James, David "Honeyboy" Edwards, Memphis Slim, and Roosevelt Sykes. Helena was also a stopping point for blues artists making their way from the Delta to Chicago.

Helena is home to the longest-running blues radio show in the world, *King Biscuit Time*, and downtown River Park is also the site of the King Biscuit Blues Festival, a four-day event held every October since 1986, which brings the blues and thousands of blues enthusiasts from around the world here to the banks of the Mississippi River.

In early 1941, blues musicians Robert Lockwood Jr. and Sonny Boy Williamson II (Rice Miller) approached Sam Anderson, the owner of KFFA,

1350 AM, Helena's first local radio station, and proposed a new blues-focused show. Anderson liked the idea and directed the duo to Max Moore, the owner of Interstate Grocery Company, distributor of King Biscuit Flour, as a potential sponsor. Moore agreed to sponsor the show if the musicians would endorse his product during commercial pauses.

From its first broadcast on November 21, 1941, to today, the thirty-minute *King Biscuit Time* showcases the best of the blues every weekday at 12:15 p.m. from KFFA radio studio in Helena. For the program's first broadcast, Williamson and Lockwood played live in the studio, becoming the original in-studio band known as the "King Biscuit Entertainers." Later, Pinetop Perkins manned the piano, and James Peck Curtis kept the beat on drums. In 1951 "Sunshine" Sonny Payne became show host, a position he would fill until he died in 2018. Blues legends from across the Delta—Muddy Waters, Little Walter, Jimmy Rogers, James Cotton, and Levon Helm—were among the featured guests.

The program's popularity solidified Helena as a major blues center and was one of the earliest integrated radio stations in the South. It reached ears within a fifty- to eighty-mile radius of Helena.

The *King Biscuit Time* program remains on the air to this day. Catch it on AM1350 Helena Monday through Friday from 12:15 p.m. to 12:45 p.m., or head to the recording studio within the Delta Cultural Center, a former train depot, to see the show in person. Benches are available for anyone who wants to sit and watch as one of the longest-running radio shows in history is recorded live.

141 Cherry St., Helena, AR; facebook.com/deltaculturalcenter

♪ MUDDY WATER'S CABIN AT THE DELTA BLUES MUSEUM
"RAINING DOWN DELTA BEATITUDE"

BORN MCKINLEY MORGANFIELD on April 4, 1913, Muddy Waters, the "father of modern Chicago Blues," was known for his glorious "raining down Delta beatitude" sound. His mother died shortly after he was born, and his grandmother, Della Grant, raised him in this wooden sharecropper's cabin on the Stovall Plantation. Grandma Grant affectionately called him "Muddy" because he loved to play in the muddy waters of nearby Deer Creek, a creek that flows from Lake Bolivar in Scott, Mississippi, south through the heart of the Mississippi Delta.

Morganfield taught himself to play harmonica here, then the guitar. He first ventured out to test his musical magic at the Stovall Plantation and, later, at local clubs.

The cabin was moved here to the Delta Blues Museum, where it was rebuilt inside to preserve Muddy Waters' launching point for generations to come.

In 1941, ethnomusicologist Alan Lomax set off in search of blues musicians across the Mississippi Delta, recording their musical genius for the Library of Congress. Lomax recorded McKinley Morganfield in this very cabin. Lomax later sent him a copy of the recording, sparking an epiphany in Morganfield as he suddenly realized his music was just as good, if not better, than tunes playing on the jukebox. "He brought his stuff down and recorded me right in my house," Waters told *Rolling Stone* magazine, "and when he played back the first song I sounded just like anybody's records. Man, you don't know how I felt that Saturday afternoon when I heard that voice and it was my own voice. Later on he sent me two copies of the pressing and a check for twenty bucks, and I carried that record up to the corner and put it on the jukebox. Just played it and played it and said, 'I can do it, I can do it.'"

Morganfield decided to finally venture out of the Delta and journey north, to Chicago, in 1943 to pursue a career as a professional musician. He would be forever known by the name his grandma bestowed upon him: Muddy Waters.

Blues fans flocked to the cabin on its original site to pay tribute to Waters, who passed away in 1983. Then a tornado blew off its roof.

Thankfully, in 1990, the House of Blues dismantled, restored, and reassembled the cabin, which is today protected within the Delta Blues Museum, the state's oldest music museum.

The museum and its extensive blues collection is housed in the circa 1918 passenger rail depot of the Yazoo and Mississippi Valley Railroad. The museum also hosts rotating exhibits and free music education for area youth.

1 Blues Alley, Clarksdale, MS; deltabluesmuseum.org

♪ STOVALL FARMS

THE MISSISSIPPI BLUES TRAIL marks Muddy Waters' original cabin location, on Stovall Farms, just outside Clarksdale: "Muddy Waters lived most of his first thirty years in a house on this site, part of the Stovall Plantation." The farmstead, which is more than 200 years old, remains in the Stovall family and is today known as Stovall Farms.

4146 Oakhurst Stovall Rd., Clarksdale, MS

♪ WROX AM
DJ SOUL MAN

FROM ITS SMALL STUDIO, located one block from the famous "Crossroads," WROX AM 1450, Clarksdale's first radio station sends the best of the best old-time hits through its airwaves to eager ears everywhere.

When it aired for the first time on June 5, 1944, the songs the station still plays today weren't considered oldies at all, as budding blues artists performed their (then contemporary) hits live on air. Among the notable guest artists here was Ike Turner, who performed solo and as a key player in Robert Nighthawk's band; Isaiah Ross, aka Doctor Ross, who played guitar, harmonica, and drums and sang; and singer and saxophonist Jackie

Brenston, who, together with Ike Turner's band, recorded "Rocket 88" in 1951. And though the *King Biscuit Time* originated at KFFA in Helena, the program was added to WROX's regular weekday schedule in the 1940s when the two stations united in a "Delta Network" so that bands had the option of broadcasting from either station.

WROX was also the home of the first Black DJ in Mississippi, Early Wright, aka "The Soul Man." Wright's "Soul Man" broadcast spanned half a century. He hosted almost every musician under the sun, including Muddy Waters, B.B. King, Sonny Boy Williamson II, Little Milton, Pinetop Perkins, Robert Nighthawk, and Tina Turner.

Wright was born on a plantation in Jefferson, Mississippi, in 1915. When he moved to Clarksdale, he was an auto mechanic intent on opening a repair shop. He also became the manager of a local gospel group called the Four Star Quartet, which had a fifteen-minute Sunday morning program.

In 1945, when Wright stopped by at WROX with the Four Star Quartet, station manager Preston "Buck" Hinman noted his charisma and offered him his own show. Wright consulted with his preacher to make sure there was nothing sinful about playing blues records on the radio, and with the holy approval, he decided to give it a go. In 1947, his nightly show, "Soul Man," featured records by blues and gospel artists both noted and undiscovered, for four straight hours. Even a young Elvis Presley appeared on Wright's show early in his career.

Wright was beloved for his folksy, unscripted banter, which included reporting church announcements and local news: "I want to let you know that some snakes has been seen in the Roundyard neighborhood. The grass has grown up around the sidewalks and snakes has been seen, looking for water. And a man told me the other day, he saw a snake in the street." He attracted a large audience, and his listeners, both Black and White, would call in to request their favorite blues, soul, gospel, and R&B songs.

Wright's show would become one of America's longest continuously running radio programs, paving the way for other African American DJs at WROX, including Ike Turner, who hosted WROX's "Jive Till Five." Wright hosted his show six days a week, almost until he died in 1999.

"I'm crazy about blues music," Wright said. "Blues is a feeling."

WROX Radio is located at 628 Desoto Ave., Clarksdale. There's also a Mississippi Blues Trail marker at 257 Delta Ave., Clarksdale, where WROX was located from 1945 to 1955.

deltaradio.net

♪ DEAK'S MISSISSIPPI SAXOPHONES & BLUES EMPORIUM
HOME OF THE HARMONICA

THE HARMONICA HAS FOUND its home in multiple musical genres: Blues, folk, classical, jazz, country, and rock feature the so-called mouth organ.

Similar mouth-blown instruments, like the Chinese sheng, have been standard in East Asia since ancient times. French Jesuit Jean Joseph Marie Amiot (1718–1793), who lived in Qing-era China, introduced the first "mouth organ" to Europe. However, German musical instrument maker Christian Friedrich Ludwig Buschmann, who also invented the accordion, is often credited with inventing the harmonica in 1821.

In 1857, German clockmaker Matthias Hohner became the first to mass-produce harmonicas. He shipped some to relatives who had emigrated from Germany to the United States, and the portable, inexpensive instrument caught on like fire across the pond. Even President Abraham Lincoln was known to carry a harmonica in his pocket.

In the early twentieth century, Southern Black musicians embraced the harmonica, bending the sound to fit the style of the "devil's music," aka the blues.

"African American traditions use a different scale than European traditions, so they could not play some of their notes on the harmonica. That is, until someone figured out that you could bend a harmonica's notes," said Barry Lee Pearson, the producer behind *Classic Harmonica Blues* (Smithsonian Folkways Recordings). "If you play a harmonica backwards—that is, suck air in, in what is now called "cross harp" or "second position"—you can take notes and force them down a pitch or two. It's really a completely different technique. It coincides with this love for instruments to sound like the voice, to make the instrument say what you say, and to make it warmer, more expressive of the voice's emotional timbres. In the blues, a harmonica can cry and whoop and holler."

Deak Harp has been playing harmonica since he was twelve, when his brother introduced him to the music of James Cotton. He eventually followed Cotton's band along the East Coast for nearly five years before Cotton offered Deak a job driving his van. Deak toured with the James Cotton Blues band for six years, sometimes joining him in the opening act and playing along with "Superharp" himself.

James Henry Cotton is best known for playing the "Blues harp," or harmonica, in Howlin' Wolf's band in the early 1950s. In 1955, he joined Muddy Waters' band before forming the Jimmy Cotton Blues Quartet, with Otis Spann on piano, in 1965.

Deak's one-man band, which combines the diddley bow, snare drum, stomp box, amplified harmonica, and vocals, became a regular feature at blues festivals and clubs in the Delta and beyond. When he's not touring the world, you can find him here, in Clarksdale, at his harmonica shop,

MERAKI ROASTING COMPANY

Meraki Roasting Company hand roasts its exceptional, small-batch coffee beans and brews them in its welcoming coffee shop. The Clarksdale company also provides young adults in the Mississippi Delta with job opportunities, hands-on training, and development with a focus on communication and entrepreneurial skill sets. Pop in for a freshly brewed cup of coffee and take a bag of Mighty Mississippi, Sunflower Soul, or Muddy Waters hand-roasted beans to go.

282 Sunflower Ave., Clarksdale, MS; merakiroasting.com

Deak's Mississippi Saxophones & Blues Emporium. The brick-and-mortar shop creates custom harmonicas to order and carries the most comprehensive selection of ready-to-play harmonicas in the world. The shop also offers harmonica repairs and harmonica lessons.

"The harmonica is the most voice-like instrument," said Charles Douglas Musselwhite, a blues harmonica player and bandleader. "You can make it wail, feel happy or cry. It's like singing the blues without words."

13 Third St., Clarksdale, MS; deakharp.com

♪ LUNATIC FRINGE LUTHIERY
MEET THE BLUES WIZARD

KEITH EDWARD KIFER, "The Blues Wizard," is a luthier, or a craftsperson who builds string instruments that have a neck and a sound box. His instruments, however, are all one-of-a-kind, since they're made from upcycled materials.

"So I wasn't using this guitar, and I thought since it wasn't hurtin' anything I might as well experiment with it," he explained to the *Ocean Beach Rag* in 2009. "I got a pan lid and a vegetable steamer rack to put in

the hole, put the strings across it, put a pick-up right in the barrel, and what I got is a sound that dobro players are jealous of."

Kifer learned instrument building from Dave Mallard, a San Diegan luthier and jazz musician. But instead of crafting his instruments of fine

Visit Clarksdale

wood, Kifer makes do with items that otherwise would have wound up in the garbage dump.

At his small shop in Clarksdale, you might find a bass guitar made with a vegetable steamer front piece or a drum set made from suitcases.

"I'm pretty sure the first dobros were made the same way," Kifer said. "Somebody stepped on a guitar and said, 'Oh my God, what am I going to do.' So they patched it with a metal bowl and played it."

247 Delta Ave., Clarksdale, MS; lunaticfringeluthiery.com

♪ HAMBONE GALLERY
FOLK ART, BEER, AND BLUES

COZY HAMBONE GALLERY brings folk art created by local artists and live music to downtown Clarksdale. They're open Tuesday through Saturday, from 11 a.m. to 5 p.m., and the gallery's popular Tuesday night concerts feature touring and local artists. The in-house Hopeless Case bar serves beer and other libations to fuel the fun. Owner Stan Street is a local folk artist and blues musician.

111 E. Second St., Clarksdale, MS; stanstreet.com

♪ BLUESBERRY CAFE
BLUES BREAKFAST

AT BLUESBERRY CAFE, breakfast comes with a side of blues.

Every Saturday and Sunday, local blues artists hit the in-cafe stage so you can sip coffee and bite into bacon, eggs, and pancakes while you soak in some of the best music in town. The intimate cafe has limited seating, so you know you'll always have a great view of the musicians onstage.

Bluesberry Cafe also hosts a blues dinner every Monday night. Dinner starts at 6:30 p.m., and the music begins at 8 p.m. Dinner specials rotate weekly, but you can expect all your Southern favorites.

235 Yazoo Ave., Clarksdale, MS; facebook.com/bluesberrycafe

♪ CAT HEAD DELTA BLUES & FOLK ART
CLARKSDALE'S BLUES AMBASSADOR

ROGER STOLLE, "Clarksdale's blues ambassador," named his record and art store Cat Head after three things: "cat head biscuits" (super-sized, fluffy Southern biscuits, as big as a cat's head), animal-themed blues record labels (Alligator, Fat Possum, Rooster, etc.), and the "cat head" drawings of Leland, Mississippi, bluesman/folk artist Pat Thomas. The shop is packed with CDs, vinyl LPs, DVDs, books, T-shirts, hats, barware, and art. Stolle and his staff offer great recommendations if you want to find out what's going on while you're in town. Local music acts often perform just outside the shop's entrance.

2534 Delta Ave., Clarksdale, MS; cathead.biz

♪ GROUND ZERO BLUES CLUB
A JUKE JOINT—INSPIRED CLUB IN THE FORMER DELTA GROCERY AND COTTON CO.

WHEN IT COMES TO THE BLUES, Clarksdale, Mississippi, is known as "ground zero"—hence the name of this juke joint–inspired club owned by Academy Award–winning actor and producer Morgan Freeman. (Freeman was born in Memphis and grew up in Charleston, Mississippi, about forty minutes southeast of Clarksdale.)

Ground Zero is housed in the former Delta Grocery and Cotton Co., a building that stood vacant for thirty years. The decor here is classic "juke joint chic": mismatched chairs and tables, Christmas lights strung up on the ceiling, and graffiti on most surfaces.

Live music is on the menu Wednesday through Saturday, as are finger-licking Southern favorites, including fried green tomatoes, catfish, hot tamales, turnip greens, and deep-fried pecan pie.

The venue also has seven apartments available for rent overnight. The apartments are located in what was once a cotton-grading warehouse. Sellers to the company brought cotton samples here to be graded visually against a skylight by cotton experts who assigned a commercial value based on the quality of the cotton. Each of the individual apartments is named after the professional term for the various assigned cotton grades: good middling, strict good ordinary, middling, strict middling, low middling, and good ordinary.

"Our mission is to showcase the best of today's Delta Blues musicians," the popular blues club declares. "Although some national acts perform from time to time, patrons are more likely to find the 'real deal' at Ground Zero Blues Club—those musicians who live in the Mississippi Delta and continue in the tradition of their musical forefathers. There is always live music Wednesday through Saturday (and even on a few Sundays when the occasion arises). We also serve a 'down home' menu that promises to please."

387 Delta Ave., Clarksdale, MS; groundzerobluesclub.com

♪ RED'S
AUTHENTIC JUKE JOINT IN THE HEART OF DOWNTOWN CLARKSDALE

RED'S LOUNGE—in the former Levine's Music Center, the shop where Ike Turner and his Kings of Rhythm bought the instruments that played the first rock 'n roll song—is an authentic juke joint, one of the few of its kind. Red's is the real deal: cash only and beer only, with a few tables and chairs scattered in the small, simple space strung with fairy lights.

What *is* a juke joint? Historians believe that the term "juke" is derived from the Gullah word for rowdy, *joog*, a word originally derived from the Wolof word *dzug*, which meant "to misconduct oneself." These community rooms, which once stood on forced labor camps across the South, were one of the few places where enslaved Black people could socialize. During Prohibition, juke joints popped up at highway crossings and railroad stops across Mississippi.

This modern-day juke joint's bluesman owner, Red Paden—who was close friends with bluesman Big Jack Johnson—offers live music. Paden learned the juke joint business from his uncle, who had a place a few miles south near the town of Alligator. Though Paden was just a little boy and thus wasn't allowed to attend any shows at his uncle's juke joints, he would crawl under the floorboards to feel the music and dancing.

"The blues is my heritage; I come up on that," Paden told NPR's Melissa Block. "Blues is something to do with the trials and tribulations that you go through. And when you can get out there and sing about it, you know, it makes the day go by quicker."

398 Sunflower Ave., Clarksdale, MS

Natalie Maynor

♪ RIVERSIDE HOTEL
WHERE BLUES GAVE BIRTH TO ROCK 'N ROLL

THE RIVERSIDE HOTEL has always been a home for wayward musical souls.

But before it was a hotel, it was a hospital.

Bessie Smith, the "Empress of the Blues" and the most popular female blues singer of the 1930s, was traveling south from Memphis on Route 61, north of the Crossroads in Clarksdale, Mississippi, with her lover, Richard Morgan. When Morgan misjudged the speed of a slow-moving truck ahead of him, he rear-ended it at a high speed. A Memphis surgeon, Dr. Hugh Smith (no relation to Bessie Smith), happened to witness this accident on September 26, 1937, and stopped to assist. He moved her to the side of the road, wrapped her arm with a handkerchief, and directed his fishing buddy to call an ambulance.

As they waited for an ambulance, yet another car approached at high speed, hitting Dr. Smith's car head-on, and sending it straight toward Bessie Smith's overturned Packard, though no one was injured in this second accident.

Finally, an ambulance arrived and transported Bessie Smith here to G. T. Thomas Afro-American Hospital, where her right arm was amputated. In shock, she had lost consciousness.

Bessie Smith died that morning, having never regained consciousness. The room where she passed on at age forty-three serves as a shrine to her spirit.

According to the Riverside Hotel's current caretaker, Zelena "Zee" Ratliff, "My grandmother had been operating the hotel since 1944. She died in the late '90s. That's when my father [Clarksdale legend Frank "Rat" Ratliff] took over the Riverside. He was only four when he walked in the door, so he remembered all the great sounds that came from each room."

The hotel was one of the few Black-owned hotels during the Jim Crow era in Mississippi. Listed in the Green Book, just about every blues and R&B great spent a night under its roof, including Sam Cooke, who many say wrote "A Change Is Gonna Come" after being inspired by the nearby Sunflower River.

It's also considered one of the birthplaces of rock 'n roll. When Ike Turner and his Kings of Rhythm, a band Turner had formed in high school, were still just a struggling R&B and soul group playing in small clubs across the South, the hotel served as their home base. They wrote and rehearsed "Rocket 88" in the hotel's basement sometime between 1949 and 1950.

THE NEGRO MOTORIST GREEN BOOK

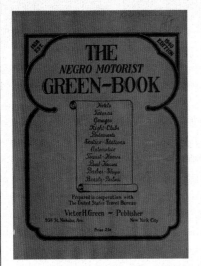

The late nineteenth and early twentieth centuries were the era of Jim Crow laws— state and local laws introduced in the South to enforce racial segregation and discrimination against African Americans. Though the emerging African American middle class was eager to hit the road, they faced a variety of inconveniences and outright danger: Some establishments refused to serve food, provide lodging, and repair vehicles for African Americans. Worse, many faced arbitrary arrest, threats of physical violence, and forcible expulsion from Whites-only "sundown towns." In 1936, Victor Hugo Green, an American postal employee and travel writer from Harlem, New York City, published *The Negro Motorist Green Book*, the first of many annual guides to the "safe" places on the road, "to give the Negro traveler information that will keep him from running into difficulties, embarrassments and to make his trip more enjoyable."

The song's unique, distorted sound was created unintentionally when the band's amplifier busted after falling off their car and onto Highway 61 as they drove through the Mississippi Delta toward Memphis. They attempted to hold the cone in place by stuffing the amplifier with wadded old newspapers, creating the unusual sound that producer Sam Phillips of Sun Studio appreciated.

At the time, "Rocket 88" was considered an R&B song, with racy lyrics that detailed sexual prowess disguised as a powerful, speeding Oldsmobile: "Everybody likes my Rocket 88; Babe we'll ride in style movin' all along; A V8 motor baby; it's modern design. Black convertible top and the girls don't mind." But its energy, driving beat, and suggestive lyrics gave it a little extra oomph that would characterize rock 'n roll.

615 Sunflower Ave., Clarksdale, MS; riversideclarksdale.com

"Down in Mississippi, where cotton grow tall,
get arrested for trouble,
you got to call the hound dog.
Oh uh, down in Mississippi, whoa yeah, where
the cotton grow tall
Yes, and on the other hand, baby, boll weevil
wearing overalls Go to work
in the morning, you know, 'bout 4 o'clock
Uh, if the mule don't holler, yeah, I don't know
when to stop
Down in Mississippi, baby, uh whoa yeah,
where the cotton grow tall
Well, and on the other hand, baby, boll weevil
wearing overalls, I go to church in the morning,
baby, you know, down the railroad track
Late over in the evening they bring, bring the
preacher back
He eat up all the chicken now, but uh right to
the neck
Look over at my baby, and he eat up all the
rest 'cause he was uh down
in Mississippi
Uh oh yeah, where the cotton grow tall
Well, now, and on the other hand, baby, boll
weevil wearing overalls.

PINETOP PERKINS, "DOWN IN MISSISSIPPI"

♪ HOPSON PLANTING COMPANY AND THE SHACK UP INN
WHERE COTTON MET THE BLUES

BY 1850, more than four million enslaved Blacks toiled on Southern cotton plantations sixteen or more hours a day. The backbreaking work in the fields was tempered by the field hands who played guitar and piano during downtime. Some of these musical workers left the cotton industry when they realized they made more money playing a Saturday evening gig than they did all week long laboring in the fields, giving them the confidence to pursue a career in the music industry. B.B. King, Son House, Muddy Waters, and Joe Willie "Pinetop" Perkins all worked as tractor drivers here at Hopson Planting Company.

Pianist Perkins worked at the Hopson Planting Company in the 1940s. On the weekends, he played at the local juke joints and was a recurring guest on the radio show *King Biscuit Time* on KFFA in Helena, Arkansas.

The Hopson Planting Company, established in 1852, was the first farm to use International Harvester cotton pickers to harvest cotton. From the 1920s through the '40s, company engineers tested and developed tractor-mounted cotton pickers in Hopson's fields and, in 1944, they succeeded in harvesting a crop using only machines. The mechanized picker could harvest a whopping six acres per day, much more than even a skilled worker could ever harvest by hand.

As the groundbreaking technology was introduced to farms across the South, the sharecropping system was replaced with wage labor, launching the "great migration" of African Americans from the Delta to northern cities as demand for manual laborers dropped.

Today, the former Hopson Planting Company Store is a lively local music venue.

Some of the sharecroppers' shacks that stood abandoned as people went north looking for work are now the unique guest rooms of the Shack Up Inn.

"Their corrugated tin roofs and Mississippi cypress walls will conjure visions of a bygone era," promises the Shack Up Inn's management. "Restored only enough to accommodate 21st-century expectations (indoor bathrooms, heat, air conditioning, coffee maker with condiments, refrigerators, and microwave in all the units), the shacks provide comfort and authenticity. As you sit in the rocker on the porch, sipping a cold one while the sun sinks slowly to the horizon, you just might hear Pinetop Perkins radiatin' the 88s over at his shack. Perhaps, if you close your eyes, even Muddy or Robert or Charlie might stop to strum a few chords in the night."

001 Commissary Circle, Clarksdale, MS; shackupinn.com

♪ W.C. HANDY ENCOUNTERS THE BLUES
"GOIN' WHERE THE SOUTHERN CROSS THE DOG"

WILLIAM CHRISTOPHER HANDY, the Father of the Blues, was waiting for a delayed train at Tutwiler's railway station when he encountered a man playing "Goin' Where the Southern Cross the Dog" on a slide guitar with a knife.

It was a moment around 1903 or 1904 that would change music history: After hearing a solitary stranger belting out the blues, Handy, who led an orchestra at the time, began incorporating blues into his musical repertoire. Eventually, in 1912, he would compose and publish "The Memphis Blues," a song that became one of the most popular blues tunes ever, introducing the world to the music of the Mississippi Delta.

Though the train station has since been demolished, its concrete foundation and floor remain.

Handy described the moment in his 1941 memoir, *Father of the Blues:*

Then, one night in Tutwiler, as I nodded in the railroad station while waiting for a train that had been delayed nine hours, life suddenly took me by the shoulder and awakened me with a start. A lean, loose-jointed Negro had commenced plunking a guitar beside me while I slept. His clothes were rags, his feet peeped out of his shoes. As he played he pressed a knife on the strings of the guitar in a manner popularized by Hawaiian guitarists who use steel bars. The effect was unforgettable. His song, too, "Goin' Where the Southern Cross the Dog."

The singer repeated the line three times, accompanying himself on the guitar with the weirdest music I had ever heard. The tune stayed in my mind. When the singer paused, I leaned over and asked him what the words meant. He rolled his eyes, showing a trace of mild amusement. Perhaps I should have known, but he didn't mind explaining. At Moorhead the eastbound and the westbound met and crossed the north and southbound trains four times a day. This fellow was going where the Southern cross the Dog, and he didn't care who knew it. He was simply singing about Moorhead as he waited.

That was not unusual. Southern Negroes sang about everything. Trains, steamboats, steam whistles, sledgehammers, fast women, mean bosses, stubborn mules—all become subjects for their songs. They accompany themselves on anything from which they can extract a musical sound or rhythmical effect, anything from a harmonica to a washboard.

In this way, and from these materials, they set the mood for what we now call blues.

♪ SONNY BOY WILLIAMSON II'S GRAVESITE

SINGER, HARMONICIST, AND SONGWRITER Sonny Boy Williamson II is buried here in a small cemetery in Tutwiler, near the tree line (GPS location N34° 01.108' W90° 27.464'). Williamson's grave was unmarked until Lillian McMurray—one of the earliest American female record producers and owner of Trumpet Records, the label that first recorded the legend in 1951—placed a tombstone in his honor in 1965. Williamson's most famous songs include "Eyesight to the Blind," "Help Me," and "Don't Start Me Talkin'."

EMMETT TILL INTERPRETIVE CENTER/ TALLAHATCHIE COUNTY COURTHOUSE

Emmett Louis Till was born and raised in Chicago. In the summer of 1955, when he was fourteen, he was visiting relatives in nearby Money, Mississippi, when he stopped at a small, local grocery store, where he encountered twenty-one-year-old Carolyn Bryant. No one except Till and Bryant knew what happened in the store, but Bryant later told her husband that Till had accosted her (later she admitted that she had made Emmett's conduct sound more threatening than it actually was).

Several nights later, Bryant's husband and his brother kidnapped Till and forced the boy to carry a seventy-five-pound cotton gin fan to the banks of the Tallahatchie River. There, the assailants ordered the boy to take off his clothes. They beat him until he was close to death, gouged out his eye, shot him in the head, tied him with barbed wire to the massive cotton gin fan, and threw him into the river.

Three days later, Till's mutilated body was recovered. His mother, Mamie Till Bradley, decided to keep her only son's casket open at his wake, which was attended by over 100,000 people over four days, so that everyone could see exactly how brutally Emmett was beaten. *Jet* magazine published the photo of the beaten and bloated child.

Bryant's husband and brother-in-law went on trial in the segregated Tallahatchie County Courthouse in Sumner, Mississippi. On September 23, 1955, the all-White, all-male jury deliberated for less than an hour before issuing a verdict of "not guilty." The two men later confessed to the kidnapping and murder but were never brought to justice.

Till's murder brought nationwide attention to racial injustice in Mississippi and beyond and catalyzed the next phase of the Civil Rights movement.

"When people saw what happened to my son, men stood up who had never stood up before," Bradley said. "People became vocal who had never vocalized before."

The Emmett Till Interpretive Center, across the street from the Tallahatchie County Courthouse, promotes "restorative justice through public education, storytelling, and historic preservation, focusing on the Emmett Till 1955 tragedy to foster community healing and understanding to create a more equitable future."

Book a tour before your visit, and plan your visit to coincide with one of the center's many educational programs.

120 N. Court St., Sumner, MS; emmett-till.org

MCCARTY'S POTTERY

NATIVE CLAY

Lee and Pup McCarty began making their famous pottery in 1954. McCarty's Pottery is beloved for its native clays and signature glazes of nutmeg brown, cobalt blue, and jade. A trademark "river" signature, a tiny, wavy line hand signed on the bottom or back of each piece, represents the Mississippi River. Known for their simple, elegant style, McCarty platters, planters, dishes, candlestick holders, and bowls are as artsy as they are useful.

Author William Faulkner played a role in the couple's early pottery success. His daughter Jill had Lee McCarty as a science teacher at a local high school in Oxford, Mississippi. The author permitted the McCartys to source clay from a ravine at the Faulkner home, Rowan Oak.

When the couple needed a home for their growing pottery business, they moved here, to Lee's hometown of Merigold, Mississippi, and set up shop in his Aunt Margaret's barn.

"We had a choice: The Cranbrook Academy of Art in California or back home," Lee McCarty told *Per/Se* magazine in 1967. "We chose home—Aunt Margaret's mule barn, in Merigold. Nailed up mattress boxes on the ceiling. Beige paint, one pint of bittersweet enamel (from Wun's, our grocer) on the barn door. Moved the kiln and wheel in. Aunt Effie wrote us up in the local paper for our own folks. We added up the leftovers and had some youth and $13.22. That was 1954."

Lee and Pup McCarty passed on in 2009 and 2015, respectively. But the McCarty Pottery tradition lives on thanks to their godchildren, Stephen and Jamie Smith.

101 St. Mary St., Merigold, MS; mccartyspottery.com

♪ PO' MONKEY'S
THE LAST OF THE RURAL JUKE JOINTS

LOCATED DOWN A GRAVEL ROAD in a sleepy, rural area adjacent to a cotton field just off Highway 61 in Merigold, Mississippi, close your eyes and try to imagine the nights when Po' Monkey's in Merigold rocked with music and dancing. The last of the rural juke joints in the Delta—named after its owner, lifelong tenant farmer Willie "Po' Monkey" Seaberry—closed in 2016. The juke joint itself, housed in circa 1920s sharecroppers' quarters, still stands as a memorial to the music that yet echoes in memory in its interior.

The joint opened back in 1963. Made of unpainted cypress planks and capped with a "tin," a corrugated galvanized steel roof, juke joints like Po' Monkey's were once a dime a dozen in the Delta. The blues grew up in joints like these before making its way to the greater American musical mindset. It's easy to imagine the humble tin and plywood quarters shaking with dirty dancing, strippers, and the blues, all fueled by $2 cans of beer sold through the small kitchen's Dutch door and the in-house DJ, an elderly man known as "Dr. Tissue," who spun the hits old and new.

Though it's now closed and eerily silent, it's still worth driving out to see the iconic juke joint, which stands as a fading memory of the days when juke joints served as entertainment hubs here in rural Mississippi.

Signs posted on its exterior reminded potential patrons of "No Loud Music, No Dope Smoking, No Rap Music."

93-99 Po Monkey Rd., Merigold, MS

PETER'S POTTERY

Peter's Pottery is a family-run pottery studio that shapes all of its beautiful pieces of pottery out of Mississippi mud, rich clay soil that reflects the rich earthy tones of the Mississippi Delta in natural colors like Dogwood Brown, Dirty Jade, Bayou Blue, and Cotton White. Visit the studio's showroom to see handcrafted vases, pitchers, mugs, bowls, platters, animal figurines, and more.

301 Fortune Ave., Mound Bayou, MS; facebook.com /peterspottery/

MOUND BAYOU

The community of Mound Bayou was founded in 1887, when former slaves led by Isaiah Montgomery and his business partner Benjamin Green cleared the 840 acres of land purchased at $7 an acre.

Montgomery's home still stands as a reminder of his legacy, as does the Bank of Mound Bayou, one of the first Black-owned banks in Mississippi. In its heyday, Mound Bayou was home to forty businesses, three cotton gins, a sawmill, a cottonseed oil mill, and a bank—all Black-owned and -managed. It was the only place in the Delta where African Americans could receive quality healthcare. The Taborian Hospital opened with great fanfare in 1942, with its all-Black medical staff of doctors and nurses; today, the Delta Health Center, which opened in 1965, provides healthcare for the community.

At a time when most Blacks in the South were working underpaid sharecropping jobs and enduring the Jim Crow South, self-sustaining and self-governing Mound Bayou was an inspiring, empowering oasis.

Start your visit to the historic town at the Mound Bayou Museum of African American Culture and History, which highlights the town's incredible history through permanent and special exhibits.

200 Roosevelt St., Mound Bayou, MS; moundbayou museum.com

♪ THE DEVIL'S CROSSROADS

TEENAGE ROBERT JOHNSON was an itinerant musician, playing juke joints across the Delta with little success.

Johnson aspired to be the greatest guitar player to walk on the Earth. However, desperation began to set in when he realized his musical ability wasn't enough. In a low moment, Johnson apparently met Satan at a crossroad, and the aspiring musician went so far as to offer his soul in exchange for extraordinary talent.

In 1930, Son House and Willie Brown played to a packed juke joint when a nineteen-year-old Johnson hit the stage to play a set at intermission, much to the crowd's displeasure. In a 1965 interview with the writer and academic Julius Lester, House recalled that Johnson "blew a harmonica and he was pretty good with that, but he wanted to play guitar," and yet when Johnson played his guitar, House urged, "Get that guitar away from that boy, he's running people crazy with it."

Johnson was so humiliated he disappeared from the music scene for about three years.

Legend states that he found himself here, at the crossroads of Highways 49 and 61, playing his guitar solo, when the Devil, under the guise of a human, took his guitar, tuned it, and then played a few songs. When the Devil handed Johnson back his guitar, he also bestowed extraordinary guitar technique on the young musician, taking his soul in exchange.

The next time Johnson returned onstage, he had nailed the blues, much to the surprise of House and Brown. "He was so good," House said. "When he finished, all our mouths were standing open."

No one could seem to explain Johnson's miraculous mastery. And thus, the devilish legend came to be.

Rolling Stones guitarist Keith Richards declared, "Robert Johnson was like an orchestra all by himself." Bob Dylan, in his *Chronicles: Volume One*, noted that Johnson's tunes "weren't customary blues songs. They were so utterly fluid. At first, they went by quick, too quick to even get. They jumped all over the place in range and subject matter, short punchy verses that resulted in some panoramic story-fires of mankind blasting off the surface of this spinning piece of plastic."

Though we may never know if Johnson made a deal with the Devil, some of the twenty-nine songs he wrote and recorded in Dallas and San Antonio from 1936 to 1937 seem to allude to a devilish encounter. In "Me and the Devil Blues," he sings, "Me and the Devil, was walkin' side by side," while in "Cross Road Blues," he sings, "I went to the crossroad, fell down on my knees/Asked the Lord above 'Have mercy, now save poor Bob, if you please.'"

Today a pole decorated with three giant blue guitars marks the exact spot where the dastardly deal allegedly went down.

599 State St. North, Clarksdale, MS

> The blues are what I've turned to, what has GIVEN ME INSPIRATION AND RELIEF IN ALL THE TRIALS OF MY LIFE.
>
> ERIC CLAPTON

♪ DOCKERY FARMS
BIRTHPLACE OF THE BLUES

ON THE BANKS of the Sunflower River, between Ruleville and Cleveland, Mississippi, Dockery Farms, a 25,600-acre cotton plantation and sawmill, is widely considered the birthplace of the blues.

In 1895, Farmer Will Dockery purchased the land for its timber but soon realized he could make more cash in cotton. He cleared and drained the land and opened it up to sharecroppers. Itinerant workers arrived from across the South, attracted by Dockery's reputation for treating his workers and sharecroppers fairly.

At its peak, the farm employed 2,000 workers, who lived on-site in boarding houses and let off steam from the daily oppression and depression by socializing and playing music in the evening hours. The "quarters" for bachelors especially attracted single, itinerant musicians and soon became known for the festive partying and music that played on deep into the night. Musicians who worked and played here include Charley Patton, Robert Johnson, Howlin' Wolf, Son House, Willie Brown, Tommy Johnson, and Pops Staples

Visitors to Dockery Farms, which is open from dawn until dusk, can stroll the farm's notable spaces, including the service station, the building that housed the cotton gin, and the Dockery Farms Baptist Church.

229 MS-8, Cleveland, MS; dockeryfarms.org

♪ CAST OF BLUES AT DELTA STATE UNIVERSITY
FACE TO FACE WITH THE BLUES

DELTA STATE UNIVERSITY, home of the "Fighting Okra," is best known for its Bologna Performing Arts Center, the sound recording studios of the Delta Music Institute, and its collection of "life casts," exact replicas of blues musicians' faces, made with damp gauze and plaster, on display in Ewing Hall.

The casts are the creation of artist Sharon McConnell-Dickerson.

When she was twenty-seven, McConnell-Dickerson woke up one morning with a vision impairment and had to leave her job as a flight attendant. A family friend brought over some clay one day. "He thought the clay would be therapeutic, and he understood that sculpture is not just about seeing," she told *St. Louis Magazine* in 2015. "My hands became my eyes. I immediately connected with the clay and decided to seek out teachers in order to begin a study of art."

McConnell-Dickerson found a new career in freehand modeling and life casting, a technique that uses molding materials to create a cast directly on the skin of a live model.

"It was just incredible for me once I was able to feel my own face after it was cast in the medium. I hadn't been able to see my face in the mirror for several years, and this life cast really captured my muscles, bones and even expressions."

She was working with the life cast method for about a year when an old friend suggested she combine her life casting talent with her love of the blues.

"He basically said to me, 'You know you do this life cast method and you're really good at it, and you also love blues music, so why don't you cast the faces of some of the blues musicians?'"

She researched blues musicians, attended blues music festivals, and began developing connections with musicians and, eventually, casting their faces.

McConnell-Dickerson invites visitors to touch the masks in this fully accessible exhibit because she wants visitors to feel what she felt in her creation process. The exhibit allows visitors to come face to face with Bobby Bland, Honeyboy Edwards, Hubert Sumlin, Bo Diddley, Othar Turner, R.L. Burnside, Little Milton, James Cotton, Johnny Winter, and more.

1003 W. Sunflower Rd., Cleveland, MS; deltastate.edu

MISSISSIPPI DELTA CHINESE HERITAGE MUSEUM

During Reconstruction, Chinese agricultural laborers, largely single men recruited by cotton planters to supplement the recently emancipated African freedmen, began immigrating to the Delta. By the end of the 1870s, Chinese had moved on from plantation work and opened grocery stores that served both Black and White patrons in the segregated South. Until the end of the 1900s, Chinese-owned grocery stores could be found in every city and small town across the Delta. Housed on the third floor of the Charles W. Capps, Jr. Archives and Museum at Delta State University, the Mississippi Delta Chinese Heritage Museum shines a spotlight on Chinese history in the region through memorabilia and photographs.

1003 W. Sunflower Rd., Cleveland, MS; chineseheritagemuseum.org

♪ GRAMMY MUSEUM MISSISSIPPI

THE MOST TECHNOLOGICALLY ADVANCED MUSIC MUSEUM IN THE SOUTH

THE GRAMMY AWARDS, presented by the Recording Academy of the United States, have recognized "outstanding" achievements in the music industry since 1959. The Grammy Museum of Mississippi, located on the campus of Delta State University, honors the award-winning artists with over 28,000 square feet packed with artifacts that tell the stories of music icons from Mississippi and beyond. It is the most technologically advanced music-themed museum in the South.

Highlights here include "On the Red Carpet," a display of the glitzy duds worn on the Grammy red carpet, and "Iconic Instruments," a brilliant display of the instruments once played by some of the world's leading musicians.

The "Mono to Surround" exhibit traces recording history, from the first recorded sound dating back to 1877, to today's high-tech transformation of sound in an acoustically enhanced room that reverberates with music.

In the Singing and Songwriting Producing Pods, visitors are invited to write and record an original blues song and then produce it via the pod's mixing capabilities.

Don't miss the Mississippi Music Bar, where visitors can listen to just about every song performed or written by iconic Mississippians, or the Mississippi Music Table, a state-of-the-art interactive exhibit where the artists seemingly float across the table.

800 W. Sunflower Rd., Cleveland, MS; grammymuseumms.org

♪ B.B. KING MUSEUM AND DELTA INTERPRETIVE CENTER
"THE BEALE STREET BLUES BOY"

RILEY B. KING was born on a cotton plantation near Itta Bena, Mississippi, on September 16, 1925. As a teen, he moved to Indianola, Mississippi. He began his career as a member of the gospel choir at a Baptist church where the minister performed with a Sears Roebuck Silvertone guitar during services and taught King his first three chords. Later, King would connect, almost spiritually, with a guitar of his own, a Gibson L-30 archtop guitar that he named Lucille. Why Lucille? Two men were fighting over a woman named Lucille at a nightclub in Twist, Arkansas, when they unintentionally knocked over a bucket of kerosene that engulfed the club in flames. King ran inside to save "her"—his guitar. He named his guitar Lucille as a reminder to "never do a thing like that again." And at times, she would "speak" from his soul.

"The minute I stop singing orally," he once said, "I start to sing by playing Lucille."

After serving in the U.S. Army, King moved to Memphis, where he found work as a radio DJ and earned the nickname B.B., aka "the Beale Street Blues Boy." Today, he's known as "The King of the Blues" for his signature tunes like "Every Day I Have the Blues," "The Thrill Is Gone," and "To Know You Is to Love You," and for shaping his electric blues style that would influence future generations of guitarists to come, including John Lennon, who once said, "I wish I could just do like B.B. King."

The B.B. King Museum and Delta Interpretive Center tells the story of King's life through artifacts, from the restored brick cotton gin building where King worked in the 1940s to the shiny 1987 Van Hool Aero Magnum tour bus that carried King and his band over twelve million miles to shows across the country between 1987 and 1992.

The museum is also King's final resting place.

When he died at age eighty-nine in 2015, he was honored with a funeral procession to the tune of "When the Saints Go Marching In" led by a brass marching band down Beale Street in Memphis. His body was then driven here down Route 61 to be buried in the museum's memorial garden. Outside, there's a life-size bronze statue of King sitting on a bench with his treasured Lucille.

400 Second St., Indianola, MS; bbkingmuseum.org

INDIANOLA PECAN HOUSE

The pecan is a nut native to the southern United States and northern Mexico. Indianola Pecan House sells fresh nuts in bulk by the pound and pecan-filled pies, pralines, cookies, truffles, and more.

1013 US-82, Indianola, MS; pecanhouse.com

♪ CLUB EBONY
THE SOUTH'S "LARGEST AND FINEST" NIGHTCLUB

ONCE UPON A TIME, Club Ebony was a vital part of the "chitlin circuit," a network of Black-owned clubs located throughout the eastern, southern, and upper Midwest areas of the United States, active during the era of racial segregation.

When the Ebony Club opened in 1948, it gave Indianola's Black community a place to gather and soak in the sounds of live acts before they hit the world stage. Ray Charles, Fats Domino, B.B. King, Count Basie, Bobby Bland, Little Milton, Albert King, Willie Clayton, and Ike

and Tina Turner all played here. Owner Johnny Jones offered a new take on the juke joint: His club was roomier, perfect for hosting the big bands of the 1940s.

"It is said to be the South's largest and finest nightclub," Jones said upon the club's opening.

B.B. King once said of Jones that he "was really the guy that kept the Negro neighborhood alive, by bringing people in, like Louis Jordan . . . Johnny Jones was a very nice fellow, and he knew the guys on the plantations didn't have any money during the week, but he would often let us in, and we would pay him off when we came on Saturday."

Today the club is managed by the B.B. King Museum, which hosts concerts and workshops in the historic venue. Check the calendar to see what's onstage at bbkingmuseum.org/event/.

404 Hanna Ave., Indianola, MS; bbkingmuseum.org

♪ CHARLEY PATTON'S GRAVESITE
FATHER OF THE DELTA BLUES

SINGER/SONGWRITER CHARLEY PATTON (1891–1934) was the quintessential itinerant Mississippi bluesman. In the 1920s and '30s, Patton rambled across the Delta and beyond. Though he didn't make his first recording until he was forty and died at forty-three, he established himself as the "Father of the Delta Blues" in his short yet enduring life.

Patton was born in Hinds County, Mississippi, in 1891, to Bill and Annie Patton, though some historians believe that Charley's biological father was actually a fiddler named Henderson Chatmon. His light complexion has led to speculation about his ancestry, and some historians believe he was part Choctaw.

In 1897, the Patton family moved to Dockery Plantation, where teenage Charley met Henry Sloan, a musician who worked as a day laborer at Dockery and was an early pioneer of the blues. Sloan mentored Patton as he entered the local music scene, playing shows at Dockery Farms and other nearby plantations.

Patton was only five feet five inches tall but boasted a husky, gravelly, far-reaching voice. His guitar skills and flashy moves drove audiences wild as he played everything from blues to ballads. He soon took his show on the road across the South and to big cities, including Chicago and New York. Willie Brown, a blues guitarist and singer also from Dockery Plantation, frequently joined Patton on the road.

In 1929, Patton recorded for the first time with Paramount Records at a studio in Indiana. His first singles include "Pony Blues," "Down the Dirt Road," and "Shake It and Break It (But Don't Let It Fall Mama)." At Paramount's studios in Grafton, Wisconsin, Patton recorded nearly thirty more songs, including "High Water Everywhere," a song that documents the Great Mississippi Flood of 1927.

He met fellow blues singer Bertha Lee at a club where he was performing, and they married soon after, in 1933.

Though their relationship would prove rocky due to Patton's alleged womanizing, she still sang on twelve of his records, including *Masters of the Delta Blues: The Friends of Charlie Patton*.

A year after they married, the couple was incarcerated in a Belzoni, Mississippi, jailhouse after a high-tempered fight. W.R. Calaway from

Vocalion Records, one of the most popular labels in the 1930s, bailed them both out of jail and brought them to New York, where Patton would record his final songs, including the prophetic "Oh Death."

While lying across Lee's lap on the Heathman-Dedham plantation near Indianola, Patton died of a heart defect on April 28, 1934.

Charley Patton's niece, Bessie Turner, recalled his death:

[He had] said, "Carry me right away from this house to the church and from the church to the cemetery." He died that Saturday, and we buried him that Sunday 'cause he didn't want to go to an undertaker. That Saturday night they had a big wake for him. A lot of his boys who sang with him was right there too. I'll never forget the last song they sung, "I'll Meet You in the Sweet Bye and Bye." They sung that so pretty and played the music, you know. Couldn't nobody cry. Everybody was just thinking how a person could change around right quick, you know. Changed right quick and then preached Revelation, the thirteenth chapter of Revelation. It says, "Let your light shine that men may see your good work and glorify our Father which art in heaven." I'll never forget it. He said, "Did you hear that? My light been shining on each side. I let it shine for the young; I let it shine for the old." Said, "Count my Christian records and count my swinging records. Just count 'em. They even!" And you know he was just smiling, just tickled to death. Looked like he was happy when he was going.

Patton was buried here, in a gravesite that remained unmarked for nearly six decades, until 1990, when musician John Fogerty erected this headstone at the New Jerusalem M.B. Church in Holly Ridge. "I was personally influenced by Howlin' Wolf," Fogerty said, "but when I discovered that Patton was the root of it all, I came here to Holly Ridge last year. It was then I first put a Patton tape in my boom box, and when I heard his voice, it sounded like Moses. I decided then I wanted to be a part of bringing recognition to this spot."

Patton's epitaph reads: "Charley Patton, the Voice of the Delta. The foremost performer of Mississippi Delta Blues, whose songs became cornerstones of American Music."

New Jerusalem Missionary Baptist Church Cemetery Holly Ridge, Holly Ridge, MS

♪ THE PEAVINE RAILROAD
PEAVINE BLUES

THE DELTA WAS BARELY NAVIGABLE, covered in swamps and forests, until the 1870s, when the railroad came to town. The Peavine Railroad, a nine-mile branch of the Yazoo and Mississippi Valley Railroad, connected Dockery Plantation (a birthplace of the blues) with the main north–south Memphis to Vicksburg rail line, popularly known as the "Yellow Dog." Bluesmen rode these rails from the late 1890s through the 1930s.

The branch, named after the pea plant's winding vines, was memorialized by Charley Patton in his 1929 song "Peavine Blues."

> I think I heard the Pea Vine when it blowed
> It blows just like my rider gettin' on board
> Well, the levee sinkin', you know I, baby . . .
> (Baby, you know I can't stay)
> The levee is sinkin', Lord, you know I cannot . . .
> I'm goin' up the country, mama, in a few more days.

Wisconsin-based Paramount Records, an American record label known for recording jazz and blues hits in the 1920s and early 1930s, used a drawing of an actual pea plant to promote Patton's record.

A historical plaque marks the spot where the Peavine rolled down the rails, at the intersection of T M Jones Highway (Mississippi Route 446) and North Tims Street, on the right, when traveling west on T M Jones Highway.

♪ LELAND MURALS
PAINTING THE GREATS

SEVERAL MURALS ON DOWNTOWN BUILDINGS of the Delta railroad town of Leland, Mississippi, depict the many greats born or raised here in the hub of Delta cotton cultivation.

The south wall of the building at the corner of Fourth and Main Streets showcases (from the top left corner of the mural) Caleb Emphrey, Sam Chatmon, Eugene Powell, Lil' Dave Thompson, Alex "Little Bill" Wallace, Eddie Cusic, Willie Foster, Johnny Horton, Joe Frank Carollo, Harry "Bub" Branton, Pat Thomas, Johnny Winter, Edgar Winter, Jimmie Reed, Boogaloo Ames, Little Milton, and James "Son" Thomas.

The west wall of the building at Third and Main Streets honors Doc's Bees, a local dance band led by "Doc" Booth on sax with Boogaloo Ames on keyboards.

"The King of the Blues," B.B. King, who hailed from nearby Indianola, is emblazoned on the south wall of the building on the corner of Third and Main Streets.

Jimmy Reed (1925–1976), who was born in Dunleith, just east of Leland, is honored with a mural on the corner of Broad Street and South Deer Creek Drive East. Reed was the bluesman behind hit songs "Honest I Do" (1957), "Baby What You Want Me to Do" (1960), "Big Boss Man" (1961), and "Bright Lights, Big City" (1961). Reed's "electric Blues" sound

was popular among the many musicians who recorded his songs, including Elvis, Hank Williams Jr., the Yardbirds, the Steve Miller Band, and the Rolling Stones.

Step inside the Leland Post Office (204 N. Broad St.) to see a New Deal–era mural, "Ginnin' Cotton," which depicts the lively mechanical process of removing gin trash—stems, burrs, and dirt—from cotton bolls and separating the cotton fibers from the seed. The mural, which was painted by Stuart R. Purser, won the 1939 48-State mural competition.

Leland, MS; highway61blues.com

THE BLUES IS CELEBRATION
because when you take sorrow and turn it into music, you transform it.
ODETTA HOLMES

THE BIRTHPLACE OF KERMIT THE FROG

Once upon a time, here on the banks of Deer Creek, a little boy dreamed up a frog that would become America's most beloved amphibian.

That boy, Jim Henson, was born in Greenville, Mississippi, in 1936 but was largely raised in Leland, Mississippi. Henson spent his childhood playing here along the frog- and turtle-filled Deer Creek. He named Kermit after his childhood buddy, Kermit Scott.

A small museum welcomes Kermit lovers from around the world with Muppet memorabilia, including an original Kermit puppet and a giant stuffed Kermit for photo ops.

Stroll across the bridge that crosses Deer Creek and see if you can spot Kermit sitting on a rock on the banks, strumming his banjo.

Who said that every wish
Would be heard and answered
When wished on the morning star?
Somebody thought of that
And someone believed it
Look what it's done so far
What's so amazing that keeps us stargazing
And what do we think we might see?
Someday we'll find it, the rainbow connection
The lovers, the dreamers, and me.

—*The Rainbow Connection*;
songwriters Paul Williams and Kenny Ascher, 1978

415 S. Deer Creek Dr. East, Leland; birthplaceofthefrog.com

WINTERVILLE MOUNDS

The Mississippi Delta is home to one of the largest and best-preserved Native American mound and plaza sites in the United States. Long, long ago—the first mound was hand-built in about AD 1100—this sacred area was an important ceremonial and political gathering place.

Of the original twenty-three large platform mounds, only twelve remain, including the 55-foot-high Temple Mound, which stands among the ten tallest mounds in the United States and is about the same height as a five-story building.

The Native Americans who lived here and built these massive mounds and grand plazas were part of the Plaquemine Mississippian culture, ancestors of the Chickasaws, Choctaws, and other Native American tribes known today. They thrived in the region from about AD 1000 to 1450, until Spaniard Hernando de Soto passed through from 1539 to 1543, introducing European diseases for which they had no immunity. By 1450, the site was abandoned altogether and recovered only when the first modern archaeological excavations, led by the National Park

Service and Harvard University's Lower Mississippi Survey, arrived here in the 1940s.

Archaeologists believe that elite tribal members lived in homes atop the mounds, with other members of the tribe living on surrounding farms where they raised the "three sisters": corn, beans, and squash.

From the top of Mound A, you can see the Mississippi River to the west.

A small museum displays the decorated pottery, stone tools, and architectural elements found on-site. A canoe on the banks of the creek that winds around the site is typical of the canoes that the Native people who lived here once used to navigate the area's many waterways.

Museum hours vary, but the mounds are open every day, from dawn to dusk.

1145 Indian Rd., Greenville, MS; mdah.ms.gov/explore -mississippi/winterville-mounds

YAZOO YAUPON

Yaupon tea is an herbal tea made from the leaves of the yaupon plant, a type of holly native to Mississippi. Native Americans used it as both a medicinal and ceremonial tea. Mild and earthy with a rich nutrient profile, yaupon tea is packed with antioxidants; some say it can help promote brain function and decrease inflammation. Oliver Luckett and his husband Scott Guinn created Yazoo Yaupon from their art-filled headquarters at 219 E. Second St. in downtown Clarksdale. Their Mississippi-made tea is available online at yazooyaupon.com and is freshly brewed locally at Meraki Roasting Company (282 Sunflower Ave., Clarksdale) and Blue Cotton Bakeshop (301 Issaquena Ave., Clarksdale).

When I'm singing the Blues,
I'M SINGING LIFE.
ETTA JAMES

DOE'S EAT PLACE

The first Italian immigrants arrived in the Mississippi Delta in the 1880s. They worked to repair levees or as farm laborers on plantations but soon became peddlers. As soon as they managed to save up enough money, they opened grocery stores, fruit stands, and eateries, despite the prejudice and discrimination they experienced due to their skin color, which was darker than those of White people of northern European heritage.

Dominick Doe Signa was born to Italian immigrant parents in 1902 in Louisiana, where his father worked in the sugar cane fields. Later the family moved here to Greenville, where they opened a grocery store, known locally as "Papa's Store." Then came the Great Flood of 1927, when the Mississippi River consumed the riverside town.

Eventually, the town rose again from the devastating floodwaters. The Signa family reopened their grocery store thanks to Big Doe Signa, who briefly entered the bootlegging biz to bring his dream of a grocery store back to life. But for this second iteration, the family transformed the front part of the store into a honky tonk. Dominick "Big Doe" Signa and his wife Mamie began serving their Italian American and local specialties to the honky tonk's patrons. Mamie cooked up Delta-style hot tamales, fried catfish, steak, and her famous salad (her secret touch was to rub the salad bowls with a garlic clove for an added kick). Word spread, and soon everyone flocked to the honky tonk to indulge in its mouth-watering steaks. Doe's Place has been racially integrated since the beginning.

Today, not only is the original Doe's Place still in the family, but the authentic eatery still serves up delicious steaks, cooked on the same grill that was specially made for Big Doe long ago; hot Delta-style tamales made following Mamie's original 1941 recipe; and housemade chili, garlic bread, and garlic-lemon-olive oil dressed salad.

502 Nelson St., Greenville, MS; facebook.com/doeseatplacegreenville/

ETHEL WRIGHT MOHAMED STITCHERY MUSEUM

Ethel Wright Mohamed, a self-taught folk artist, "painted" her life in thread. Born on a farm in Webster County, Mississippi, in 1906, she started working at age fifteen at a local bakery. One day, a young, handsome, local dry goods merchant named Hassan Mohamed purchased fresh bread. The two fell in love, and despite their different religious backgrounds—Hassan was Muslim while Ethel's father was a lay Baptist minister—they married and built a family together. But then Hassan passed away, and their eight children eventually flew the coop of home. So she set out to preserve her memories in stitches. "I felt as if I was like a big ship floating around without any reason or any purpose, but one thing I had was a lot of beautiful memories," she said. "I wished I could live my life over. Of course, I couldn't do that. I thought, if I could write, I would write a book. I tried my hand at painting but painting wasn't it. So, I decided to stitch a while. Sitting in my rocking chair, I got my needle and thread out and it was just the thing for me."

This unique museum, open by appointment only, showcases hundreds of Mohamed's "memory pictures" and is housed in her former home. Curator Carol Mohamed Ivy (daughter of Ethel Wright Mohamed) guides visitors through the exhibit while also sharing fascinating family stories hidden among the stitches.

307 Central Ave., Belzoni, MS; mamasdreamworld.com

> Every bad situation is a **BLUES SONG WAITING TO HAPPEN.**
>
> AMY WINEHOUSE

CATFISH FESTIVAL

Mississippi has led the country in catfish ever since Mississippians began commercially producing catfish around 1965, and the bottom feeders are featured on menus at many a Mississippi restaurant. The town of Belzoni, which lies between the Mississippi and Yazoo Rivers, is the catfish capital of the state. Belzoni hosts the annual World Catfish Festival each spring.

belzonims.com/catfishfest.htm

♪ BLUE FRONT CAFE
THE OLDEST SURVIVING JUKE JOINT IN MISSISSIPPI

CAREY AND MARY HOLMES, an African American couple from Bentonia, opened the Blue Front Cafe in 1948 as a side gig to supplement their income as cotton farmers.

The cafe soon developed a reputation for the blues, buffalo fish, and corn-made moonshine. Workers from the surrounding Yazoo County farms flocked to the cafe in the evening hours for a hot meal and sometimes even a haircut in the cafe that doubled as a community space. Although Black-owned businesses were subject to a 10 p.m. curfew and could not serve Coca-Cola, the Blue Front Cafe sometimes stayed open 24/7 to accommodate second- and third-shift farm laborers, and served Nehi and Double Cola in addition to its coveted corn whiskey.

The cafe was so successful that the Holmeses raised their ten children, three nephews, and four grandchildren and sent many off to college on the income generated by the cafe and their cotton crops.

MISSISSIPPI PETRIFIED FOREST

Thirty-six million years ago, 100-foot-tall fir and maple trees were toppled by a storm, then washed down an ancient roaring river here in Flora, Mississippi. They landed in the riverbanks, where sand and silt buried them. Then they began to decay. Ever so slowly, the organic materials in the trees' cell walls were replicated with minerals, transforming them into stone logs via a process called petrification. One of only two petrified forests in the eastern United States, the Mississippi Petrified Forest was declared a National Natural Landmark in 1965.

A self-guided, paved trail meanders among the ancient trees. An earth science museum here showcases fossils, petrified wood, and minerals from around the world, including a complete cast of a prehistoric camel.

124 Forest Park Rd., Flora, MS; mspetrifiedforest.com

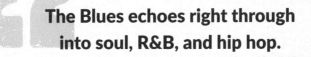

> ## The Blues echoes right through into soul, R&B, and hip hop.
> ## It's part of the makeup of modern music.
> ## YOU CAN'T TURN YOUR BACK ON THE BLUES.
> ## RONNIE WOOD, THE ROLLING STONES

Despite never booking or advertising in-cafe entertainment, the list of itinerant blues musicians who popped in to play at this stageless cafe reads like a who's who listing of famous players: Jack Owens, Henry Stuckey, Sonny Boy Williamson II (Rice Miller), James "Son" Thomas, Bud Spires, Son Johnson, Bobby Batton, Alonzo (Lonzy) Wilkerson, Cleo Pullman, Cornelius Bright, Jacob Stuckey, Dodd Stuckey, and Tommy Lee West.

Bentonia local Nehemiah "Skip" James often played guitar and piano here. His "22-20 Blues," recorded in 1931, inspired Robert Johnson's "32-20 Blues" of 1936.

When Carey Holmes died in 1970, his son Jimmy "Duck" Holmes took over the Blue Front Cafe. Duck grew up soaking in the blues. He has recorded a few albums at the Blue Front Cafe with Blue Front Records (bluefrontrecords.com). His 2019 recording "Cypress Grove" was nominated for the Grammy Award for Best Traditional Blues Album in 2021. Despite this, he doesn't write music or lyrics or even read music. "I mean, I guess it's a divine thing," he told CBS News in 2021. "I don't know."

107 W. Railroad Ave., Bentonia, MS; facebook.com/bluefrontcafeblues

♪ FARISH STREET HISTORIC DISTRICT

BLACK MECCA OF MISSISSIPPI

THE 125-ACRE FARISH STREET HISTORIC DISTRICT was born during Reconstruction and constructed by Black Mississippians as a neighborhood where they could build their own homes and businesses during the Jim Crow era when they were banned from working in White-controlled areas of Jackson. It was once considered the "Black mecca of Mississippi." In its mid-twentieth-century heyday, it stood as the largest economically independent Black community in Mississippi, its streets bustling with passersby, music echoing from its many clubs, theaters, and recording

studios. Trumpet Records, Ace Records, and the Speir Phonograph Company were all born in this progressive, musical district.

"Much of the crowd then consisted of country folks who took special buses to Farish Street to stock up on dry goods and visit the cafes on the street, where beer flowed inexpensively, and jukeboxes blared out the latest R&B sounds," blues scholar Scott Barretta wrote in *Farish Street Blues: Rebuilding A "Music Town"* (Jackson Free Press, 2004). "The records themselves could be bought at several local furniture stores, including one that contained a recording studio and nationally distributed label, while moviegoers could choose from the selections at the Amite, the Booker T, and the Alamo; the latter also hosted prominent out-of-town touring bands."

Since 1915, the **Alamo Theatre** (333 N. Farish St., Jackson, MS; facebook.com/thealamotheater) has presented everything from piano-accompanied silent movies to talkies to music talent shows to blues and jazz concerts by artists such as Nat "King" Cole, Elmore James, Louis Jordan, the Southern Sons, and Cab Calloway to gospel groups.

> **The Blues are the roots, and the other musics are the fruits. It's better keeping the roots alive, because it means better fruits from now on. THE BLUES ARE THE ROOTS OF ALL AMERICAN MUSIC.** As long as American music survives, so will the Blues.
>
> WILLIE DIXON

Dorothy Moore was offered a recording contract after appearing in a talent show hosted here.

Moore, best known today for her 1976 record *Misty Blue*; her hit songs "Funny How Time Slips Away," "I Believe You," and "With Pen in Hand"; and for leading The Poppies, an R&B/pop group behind the 1966 hit "Lullaby of Love."

The theater still presents occasional performances and movie screenings.

Countless musicians traveled the Greyhound bus, including American Delta Blues singer, songwriter, and guitarist Arthur Crudup, who sang "Greyhound Bus Blues." The **Old Greyhound Bus Depot** (219 N. Lamar St., Jackson, MS), a masterpiece of Art Deco architecture, stands today as a visible reminder of the many arrests made here during the May 1961 Freedom Rides of the Civil Rights movement.

Cap off your visit to the historic district at the **Big Apple Inn** (509 N. Farish St.; facebook.com/bigappleinn/), an eatery renowned for its delectable pig ear and smoked sausage sandwiches.

Amite Street across to Fortification Street and Mill Street to Lamar Street, Jackson, MS; visitjackson.com/directory/farish -street-historic-district

HAL & MAL'S
JACKSON'S MUSICAL GATHERING PLACE

IN THE EARLY 1980s, brothers Harold and Malcolm White, better known as Hal and Mal, were living in New Orleans, working as a chef and assistant general manager, respectively, at the Bourbon Orleans Hotel, when they devised a plan: to create a gathering place in Jackson.

Since the duo opened Hal & Mal's in 1985, the bar and restaurant has brought music lovers and musical artists together, including Albert King, B.B. King, Koko Taylor, Little Milton, Mose Allison, James Brown, Johnny Winter, R.L. Burnside, Bobby Rush, and The Temptations, as well as newer performers such as The Strokes and Snoop Dog.

Try the house specialties like Myrtis Bayou gumbo, named after the brothers' Aunt Myrtis, who trapped crabs in Mary Walker Bayou near Gautier, Mississippi. But stay for the music, onstage most days of the week.

200 Commerce St., Jackson, MS; halandmals.com

♪ ROBERT JOHNSON HOUSE

BLUESMAN ROBERT JOHNSON was born in this tiny wooden home on the outskirts of Hazlehurst, Mississippi, on May 8, 1911. Though he spent much of his childhood in Memphis, he returned to Hazlehurst in the early 1930s, where Isaiah "Ike" Zimmerman mentored him. One of Zimmerman's daughters, interviewed by blues researcher Bruce Conforth (*Ike Zimmerman: The X in Robert Johnson's Crossroads Living Blues*, 2008), recalled Johnson playing along with her father:

> Robert Johnson asked my daddy to teach him how to play guitar . . . and my daddy taught him. He lived there with my daddy . . . he stayed a long time . . . he was staying to learn how to play the guitar. . . . It seemed like to me he just took him for his family 'cause . . . for a long time I thought he was related. . . . And they was going at that guitar like some . . . I told my son, "I can remember hearing that music." 'Cause it sounded just so good just like they was competing, he was teaching him then.

The house was moved from its original location on Damascus Road to Miller Road when Highway 55 was constructed. Today the house is on the Heritage House Cultural Center site in downtown Hazlehurst.

201 Downing St., Hazlehurst, MS; heritagehousecopiah.org

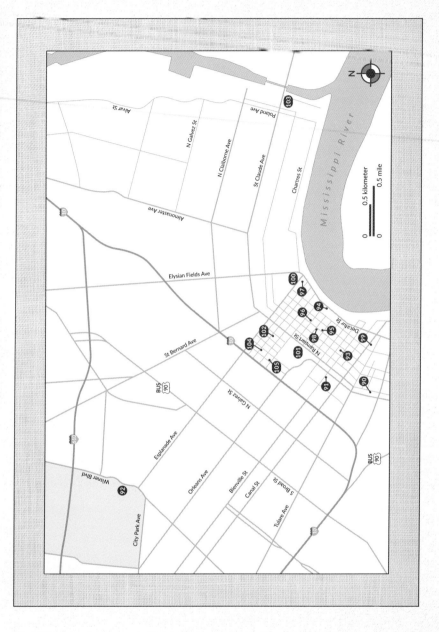

NEW ORLEANS

♪ EAGLE SALOON
LITTLE LOUIS ARMSTRONG'S HAUNT

AMERICAN TRUMPETER AND VOCALIST Louis Armstrong was among the most influential figures in jazz. Likely born on August 4, 1901, in New Orleans, he grew up in poverty in this neighborhood known then as the Battlefield or the Back o' Town.

From the turn of the century through the 1920s, the Battlefield was a rough and tough area of town, a red-light district brimming with brothels and saloons. Armstrong soaked in the early sounds of jazz at the neighborhood social halls, dance clubs, cabarets, and vaudeville theaters.

Most of the structures that stood during Armstrong's childhood have been torn down, but the Eagle Saloon still stands on the corner of Perdido Street.

Close your eyes and imagine the days when music by jazz pioneers Jelly Roll Morton, who published one of the first jazz compositions, "Jelly Roll Blues," in 1915, and Buddy Bolden, considered one of the first and most influential jazz musicians, streamed from the Eagle Saloon's windows into the streets.

On New Year's Eve 1913, a young Louis Armstrong shot a pistol into the air in front of the Eagle Saloon. He was arrested and sentenced to eighteen months at the regrettably named Colored Waif's Home, a spartan juvenile detention facility on the outskirts of New Orleans, where corporal punishment was common and meals sparse. Despite this, Armstrong was able to hone his cornet skills by playing in the facility's brass band. Peter Davis, a warden who also directed the youth band, became Armstrong's first formal music teacher.

The neoclassical Eagle Saloon is currently vacant, anxiously waiting the chance to be lovingly restored back to life.

401 S. Rampart St., New Orleans

> On Liberty, Perdido, Franklin, and Poydras, there were honky tonks at every corner, and in each one, instruments of all kinds was played. At the corner of the street where I lived was the Famous Funky Butt Hall where I first heard Buddy Bolden play. **HE WAS BLOWING UP A STORM.**
> LOUIS ARMSTRONG,
> SATCHMO: MY LIFE IN NEW ORLEANS, 1954

♪ FRANK EARLY'S MY PLACE SALOON
STORYVILLE

STORYVILLE WAS YET ANOTHER legendary red-light district in early 20th-century New Orleans.

Prostitution was the main draw to Storyville, while jazz musicians fueled the scene with music at the neighborhood's many brothels. Dance halls and cabarets provided entertainment into the wee hours.

The so-called *Blue Book*, first published in 1895, was created to advertise the various services of the sex workers of Storyville, the only neighborhood in town where prostitution was tolerated, thanks to City Councilman Sidney Story. Inspired by German and Dutch red-light ports, Story drafted legislation that detailed guidelines for prostitution within the neighborhood's limits, even though it was still technically illegal.

Madams hired musicians to entertain clients. And since the clients weren't coming to the brothels solely for the music, performers could experiment with their musical styles.

Jelly Roll Morton recalled:

> If a Naked Dance was desired, Tony [Jackson] would dig up one of his fast-speed tunes and one of the girls would dance on a little narrow stage, completely nude. Yes, they danced absolutely stripped, but in New Orleans the Naked Dance was a real art. . . . Not all the piano players in the District were of the type and class as Tony Jackson. At the time, back in 1901, and 1902, we had a lot of great Blues players that didn't know nothing but the Blues. . . .

Tony Jackson was a ragtime pianist who played here before he moved to Chicago in the mid-1910s. Perhaps best known for his 1916 song "Pretty Baby," which likely referred to his male lover—Jackson was openly gay—Jackson was known as a "piano professor," the term for pianists who could cover just about any song request, no matter the genre.

Most of Storyville's historic structures were demolished to make way for the Iberville public housing project in the 1940s. Six original structures and remnants remain, including Frank Early's My Place Saloon here at 1216 Bienville St., though today it's a grocery shop. The other two surviving buildings are Joe Victor's Saloon at 1534 St. Louis St. and the first floor of Lulu White's Saloon at 237 Basin St., which once catered to some of the most prominent and wealthiest men in town and was owned by Madame Lulu White, "The Queen of Storyville," who dripped in jewelry.

> # POETRY, LIKE JAZZ, IS ONE OF THOSE DAZZLING DIAMONDS
> ## of creative industry that help human beings make sense out of the comedies and tragedies that contextualize our lives.
>
> ### ABERJHANI, JOURNEY THROUGH THE POWER OF THE RAINBOW: QUOTATIONS FROM A LIFE MADE OUT OF POETRY

♪ SINGING OAK
"LET THE WIND BRING YOU A MELODY"

NEW ORLEANS IS SUCH A historical, musical city that even its trees sing: Located on the south side of City Park, just east of Big Lake, the so-called Singing Oak, or Chime Tree, goes beyond providing shade by also "singing," thanks to the tens of wind chimes that dangle from its branches.

Local artist Jim Hart designed and installed the chimes that adorn the majestic, century-old towering oak tree. Hart painted them flat black, so they would blend in with the trees' leaves, making it appear that the tree is truly singing solo, and tuned them to ring out in the pentatonic scale, featuring five notes per octave, characteristic of West African gospel hymns and New Orleans jazz.

A plaque at the tree's base reads: "Let the wind bring you a melody, a smile and a sense of peace and nature."

1701 Wisner Blvd., New Orleans

Richard Weaver

♪ MUSICAL LEGENDS PARK
A MUSICAL OASIS ON BOURBON STREET

THOUGH IT WAS NAMED FOR the French royal family and not the barrel-aged American whiskey, Bourbon Street has long been a place where revelry is fueled by liquor and music. Running thirteen blocks through the heart of the French Quarter, from Canal Street to Esplanade Avenue, the monumental street dates back to 1718, when Jean-Baptiste Le Moyne de Bienville, a French colonial administrator in New France, founded New Orleans.

In the late 1800s, the raucous nightlife of Storyville, the adjacent red-light district, began seeping into what was initially a residential neighborhood; by the 1950s, cabarets, strip joints, bars, and clubs lined the street.

A small park on Bourbon Street, the New Orleans Musical Legends Park, stands as an oasis from the revelry of Bourbon Street, centered by a bubbling fountain, with tables and chairs to welcome weary passersby. The park is overseen by life-size statues of the music legends who once

Visit New Orleans

played at the surrounding nightclubs: Antoine Fats Domino on piano, Al Jumbo Hirt and Louis Primo on trumpet, and Pete Fountain on clarinet. Irma Thomas, "Soul Queen of New Orleans," and Chris Owens, host of the Chris Owens Review cabaret act, sing in perfect silent harmony. New Orleans–based jazz pianist Ronnie Kole raises a glass of champagne.

Best of all, the park hosts live jazz daily, from 10 a.m. to close.

311 Bourbon St., New Orleans; neworleansmusicallegends.com

CAFÉ DU MONDE

Creoles descended from the inhabitants of colonial Louisiana began mixing their coffee with chicory during the Civil War when coffee was scarce. Chicory adds a woody, nutty flavor. Café du Monde, since it was founded in 1862, has been selling two treats that showcase New Orleans' rich history: delectable, pillowy beignets (fried dough generously dusted with powdered sugar) paired with rich café au lait made with dark coffee and chicory. Café du Monde is open 24 hours a day, every day, except for Christmas.

800 Decatur St., New Orleans; cafedumonde.com

♪ PRESERVATION HALL
LIVE JAZZ, 350 NIGHTS A YEAR

PRESERVATION HALL, a concert hall in the heart of the French Quarter, has been echoing with New Orleans–style jazz since it opened in 1962 as a safe space for jazz musicians to perform during a time when state laws still prohibited interracial performances (Jim Crow laws would not be entirely overturned until the Civil Rights Act of 1964 and the Voting Rights Act of 1965.)

In the 1950s, Larry Borenstein, an art dealer from Milwaukee, managed a gallery here at 726 St. Peter St. But Borenstein soon realized he was missing out on too many concerts, so he began inviting local jazz musicians to perform "rehearsal sessions" in his gallery. When the music began overshadowing the art, it became "Preservation Hall."

NEW ORLEANS HISTORIC VOODOO MUSEUM

New Orleans Voodoo is a religion connected to nature, spirits, and ancestors. Enslaved West Africans brought their traditional beliefs with them to Louisiana, where their rituals and practices merged with the Roman Catholicism of the French. Later, elements of Haitian Voodoo were added as Haitian migrants fled to Louisiana following the Haitian Slave Revolt of 1791.

New Orleans Voodoo is centered on the belief that although God does not interfere in our daily lives, a myriad of spirits do.

Though small in size, the New Orleans Historic Voodoo Museum has taken on the big job of unpacking the myths and truths that surround the city-born religion with its collection of ritual Voodoo objects—taxidermy, talismans, gris-gris dolls, and even the prayer bench of renowned local Voodoo practitioner healer and herbalist Marie Laveau— from New Orleans and beyond.

Visit New Orleans

On-site Voodoo priests and priestesses offer spiritual readings, and the museum also hosts tours of local cemeteries, including tours of St. Louis Cemetery No. 1, the oldest and among the most prominent cemeteries in New Orleans since it opened in 1789.

Some followers of Louisiana Voodoo still pray to Laveau, some even try to channel her, and many leave offerings at her suspected final resting spot at St. Louis Cemetery No. 1 (plot 37). The Archdiocese of New Orleans closed the cemetery to the public in 2015 to protect its eighteenth- and nineteenth-century tombs, but you can take an official guided tour.

724 Dumaine St., New Orleans; voodoomuseum.com

In 1961, Allan Jaffe and his wife Sandra were on their honeymoon in New Orleans when they bumped into local musicians who introduced them to the hidden gem of a venue. The couple was so enamored with the French Quarter that they agreed when Borenstein asked if they wanted to manage Preservation Hall

Jaffe made a point of hiring local, older musicians, many of whom were struggling with poverty. Even though the Jaffes served no alcohol, used no amplification, and did not advertise, fans began pouring in from all over the world to hear traditional jazz at Preservation Hall.

The charming, classic Creole-style building it's housed in, with its board and batten shutters, French doors, and iron gates, has been largely unaltered since it was built in 1817. Imagine the early days when horses and carriages passed through its *porte-cochère* (coach door) leading into the interior courtyard.

Preservation Hall hosts live jazz concerts 350 nights a year.

726 St. Peter St., New Orleans; preservationhall.com

THE NEW ORLEANS JAZZ MUSEUM AT THE OLD U.S. MINT

CELEBRATING JAZZ IN THE CITY WHERE THE MUSICAL GENRE WAS BORN

THE NEW ORLEANS MINT produced over 427 million gold and silver coins in the nineteenth and early twentieth centuries. The Greek Revival–style building, long decommissioned as a mint, now houses the New Orleans Jazz Museum in the city where jazz was born.

The museum celebrates jazz through listening stations, a recording studio, and a comprehensive collection of jazz artifacts, including the world's most extensive collection of jazz instruments played by the greats, 12,000 photographs from the early days of jazz, over 4,000 78 rpm records that date from 1905 to the mid-1950s, and hundreds of pieces of first-edition sheet music ranging from late nineteenth-century ragtime to popular songs of the 1940s and '50s.

On the museum's third floor, the Performance Center comes alive almost every day of the week with jazz concerts, theatrical performances, symposia, workshops, lectures, or jazz yoga for health-minded jazz enthusiasts.

400 Esplanade Ave., New Orleans; nolajazzmuseum.org

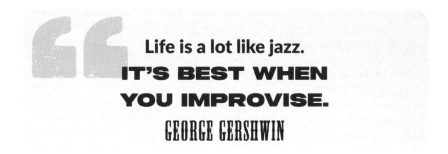

Life is a lot like jazz.
IT'S BEST WHEN
YOU IMPROVISE.
GEORGE GERSHWIN

♪ FRITZEL'S JAZZ PUB
OLDEST OPERATING JAZZ CLUB IN NEW ORLEANS

FRITZEL'S JAZZ CLUB was founded in 1969 in an 1831 building with a traditional French Quarter–style balcony. The club's house band plays traditional New Orleans jazz music daily starting at 8 p.m.

733 Bourbon St., New Orleans; fritzelsjazz.com

Gary Brownell

> There's something beautifully friendly and elevating about a bunch of guys playing music together. This wonderful little world that is unassailable. **IT'S REALLY TEAMWORK**, one guy supporting the others, and it's all for one purpose, and there's no flies in the ointment, for a while. And nobody conducting, it's all up to you. It's really jazz ... that's the big secret. **ROCK AND ROLL AIN'T NOTHING BUT JAZZ WITH A HARD BACKBEAT.**
> KEITH RICHARDS, LIFE

HOUSE OF SAZERAC

Sazerac, perhaps the oldest American cocktail—a combination of cognac or rye whiskey, absinthe, Peychaud's Bitters, and sugar—was named for its main ingredient, the Sazerac de Forge et Fils brand of cognac.

Around 1850, Sewell T. Taylor sold his New Orleans bar, the Merchants Exchange Coffee House, to become an importer of Sazerac de Forge et Fils cognac. Meanwhile, Aaron Bird assumed ownership of the Merchants Exchange, changed its name to Sazerac Coffee House, and began serving cocktails that mixed the brand-name cognac with bitters supplied by a local apothecary, and the Sazerac cocktail was born.

The Sazerac House is located just a few hundred yards from the original site of the Sazerac Coffee House, where the cocktail was first served. This tourist attraction immerses visitors in New Orleans cocktail culture with cutting-edge exhibit technology that simulates the French Quarter in the 1800s. Admission is complimentary, but you need to reserve tickets online in advance.

101 Magazine St., New Orleans; sazerachouse.com

♪ LOUISIANA MUSIC FACTORY
WHERE VINYL IS STILL KING

VINYL STILL REIGNS SUPREME at Louisiana Music Factory, one of the biggest and best shops in New Orleans, known for its fine selection of new and used vinyl. If you're looking for that rare, obscure jazz record, you just might find it here. The LMF, as it's known locally, also transforms into a live music venue, regularly hosting local jazz and Cajun artists and streaming its sessions on its YouTube channel at youtube .com/user/lamusicfactory

421 Frenchmen St., New Orleans; louisianamusicfactory.com

> **I'M ALWAYS THINKING ABOUT CREATING.** My future starts when I wake up in the morning and see the light.
> ## MILES DAVIS

♪ CONGO SQUARE IN LOUIS ARMSTRONG PARK
NEW ORLEANS' HISTORIC MUSICAL GATHERING SPACE

AMIDST THE BUSTLING French Quarter, within Louis Armstrong Park, Congo Square has stood as a musical gathering place since New Orleans was but a baby. Congo Square is perhaps the true birthplace of jazz.

Once a week, enslaved peoples of Africa and free Creoles of color sang and danced here at this site, one of the rare places where they could congregate and trade in goods and ideas. They carried traditional

instruments—drums, gourds, pan flutes made of reeds, as well as European instruments like the violin—and added the rhythms and syncopation of their native lands to the mix. They danced, sang, and played music together—music that contained the core elements of jazz.

Congo Square continues to be a community gathering space, hosting musical performances and other celebratory events. Every Sunday, the Congo Square Preservation Society, a community-based organization created by percussionist Luther Gray, carries on the tradition of gathering in historic Congo Square to celebrate the people who gathered here long before us, through drum circles, dancing, and other musical performances.

701 N. Rampart St., New Orleans; congosquarepreservation society.org

Visit New Orleans

SAINT AUGUSTINE CATHOLIC CHURCH

SITE OF THE INFAMOUS "WAR OF THE PEWS"

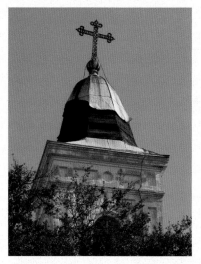

Established in 1841, St. Augustine Church is the oldest Black Catholic parish in the nation.

Formerly enslaved residents organized and received permission from the bishop to build a church of their own on the site of the Claude Treme plantation. At a time when the Catholic Church charged a fee just to sit in the pews, the same free people of color who organized to build the church organized to pay for extra pews so that enslaved Blacks could also attend mass, leading to the so-called War of the Pews.

According to the church's website: "Upon hearing of this, white people in the area started a campaign to buy more pews than the colored folks. Thus, The War of the Pews began and was ultimately won by the free people of color who bought three pews for every one purchased by the whites. In an unprecedented social, political, and religious move, the colored members also bought all the pews of both side aisles. They gave those pews to the slaves as their exclusive place of worship, a first in the history of slavery in the United States. This mix of the pews resulted in the most integrated congregation in the entire country: one large row of free people of color, one large row of whites with a smattering of ethnicities, and two outer aisles of slaves. Except for a brief six-month period when its sanctuary was being enlarged and blessed in time for Christmas, Saint Augustine Church has been in continuous use as a place of worship. We celebrate our Anniversary every October."

1210 Governor Nicholls St., New Orleans; staugchurch.org

> **JAZZ IS THE ONLY** unhampered, unhindered **EXPRESSION OF COMPLETE FREEDOM** yet produced in this country.
>
> DUKE ELLINGTON

♪ MUSIC BOX VILLAGE
MUSICAL ARCHITECTURE

THE MUSIC BOX VILLAGE is an ever-evolving art installation billed by its artist collective New Orleans Airlift as "musical architecture." At least sixteen "musical houses" immersed in a wooded slice of green space make for an interactive, outdoor "sonic sculpture" as they each play their unique melody. The result is a mystical harmony that's never quite the same.

The outdoor venue also hosts a series of concerts and workshops and has a full bar.

The Music Box Village has a limited schedule of performances and is open only during scheduled events, so check the online event calendar before you go.

4557 N. Rampart St., New Orleans; musicboxvillage.com

♪ TREME'S PETIT JAZZ MUSEUM
COZY MUSEUM WITH A COOL COLLECTION

FOUNDED IN THE 1810s when a former plantation was subdivided and sold to a diverse population, Treme is one of the oldest neighborhoods in New Orleans and the oldest African American neighborhood in the nation.

The Storyville red-light district was once a part of the mixed-race neighborhood, and the music that grew from its nightclubs reflected its rich blend of musical heritages and cultural expressions.

Al Jackson, a Treme native, spent decades studying New Orleans' music history before opening this charming, cozy museum to display his personal collection of archival photographs, vintage instruments, art, and artifacts, including performing contracts for soon-to-be-world-famous musicians such as Fats Domino and Little Richard.

Jackson is often present at this museum, eager to share his vast knowledge of jazz and its ties to the Treme neighborhood.

1500 Governor Nicholls St., New Orleans; facebook.com/tremespetit jazzmuseum

> And that's the soulful thing about playing: **YOU OFFER SOMETHING TO SOMEBODY.** You don't know if they'll like it, but you offer it.
>
> WYNTON MARSALIS, TO A YOUNG JAZZ MUSICIAN: LETTERS FROM THE ROAD

♪ BACKSTREET CULTURAL MUSEUM

CELEBRATING TRADITIONS YOU'LL ONLY FIND IN NEW ORLEANS

THE BACKSTREET CULTURAL MUSEUM is dedicated to the colorful traditions you'll only find in the rich melting pot that is the city of New Orleans. Housed in the former Blandin Funeral Home, the small museum features exhibits on the social aid and pleasure clubs, jazz funerals,

Visit New Orleans

balls, and Carnival traditions that make the city so unique. Per the museum's website: "The exhibits illuminate African American history in the struggles against slavery and disenfranchisement and for freedom. The artisans who created the objects know hardship, yes. But they also know how to live triumphantly and express the beauty of life, something that no hardship can ever take away."

One highlight here is the brilliantly colored, elaborate Mardi Gras Indian costumes, the city's largest collection. Handmade by local artisans, the costumes are adorned with beads, stones, shells, rhinestones, sequins, and feathers and can cost upwards of $10,000 apiece, typically take over a year to create, and can only be worn during the year they were made.

1116 Henriette Delille St., New Orleans; backstreetmuseum.org

SUGGESTED ITINERARY AND TRAVEL TIPS

This itinerary highlights the most important historic, music-related sites easily accessible from the route that runs from Nashville to New Orleans and along the fabled Blues Highway, Route 61, through the Mississippi Delta. It also veers off course toward lesser-known sights and sounds. Beyond the curated list of the most iconic sights to see on this musical journey, expect to discover other hidden gems along what will no doubt be the road trip of a lifetime.

GETTING AROUND Fly into Memphis International Airport, or reverse the itinerary and fly into New Orleans (Louis Armstrong International Airport). You'll need a car to explore the more off-the-beaten-path sites featured in this book; car rentals are available at both airports.

WHERE TO SLEEP Roadside motels and hotels (e.g., EconoLodge, Motel 6, Quality Inn) abound along the route. If you're looking for a more history-filled stay, see suggestions below.

 **ROAD TRIP SOUNDTRACK** No road trip is complete without a soundtrack: Check out the QR code to a curated Spotify list of songs related to historic sites featured in this travel guide. In the Delta, tune into WDSW The Trail (WDSW-LP), Delta State University's campus radio station, which features a delightful mix of folk, blues, and rock and also streams worldwide via the TuneIn service available on your Alexa device.

UPDATED TRAVEL INFORMATION For updated travel information, check in with the local or state tourist boards.

- Tennessee Department of Tourism, tnvacation.com
- Visit Mississippi, visitmississippi.com
- Explore Louisiana, explorelouisiana.com

DAY 1 NASHVILLE

- ★ Country Music Hall of Fame and Museum
- ★ Hatch Show Print
- ★ Johnny Cash Museum
- ★ Patsy Cline Museum
- ★ The Gibson Garage
- ★ Settle in for the Bluegrass Jam at the Station Inn

⚲ WHERE TO STAY IN NASHVILLE

GRADUATE NASHVILLE, graduatehotels.com/nashville

THE RUSSELL, russellnashville.com

DREAM NASHVILLE, dreamhotels.com/nashville

DAY 2 NASHVILLE

- ★ Gruhn Guitars
- ★ Enjoy a performance at the Ryman Auditorium or catch live music at Nudie's Honky Tonk and Tootsie's Orchid Lounge
- ★ Celebrate Dolly Parton with a late-night cocktail at White Limozeen

DAY 3 NASHVILLE

- ★ National Museum of African American Music
- ★ Stroll the Historic Center of Nashville's African American Community (Rosa Parks Boulevard and Jefferson Street)
- ★ Catch a show at Bluebird Cafe or Grand Ole Opry Live

DAY 4 **NASHVILLE TO MEMPHIS**

- ★ Tina Turner's Schoolhouse and the home of "Sleepy" John Adam Estes (West Tennessee Delta Heritage Center)
- ★ Billy Tripp's Mindfield
- ★ Lunch at Helen's BBQ
- ★ Lauderdale Courts Apartments
- ★ Sun Studio
- ★ Stroll Beale Street

♥ WHERE TO STAY IN MEMPHIS

GUEST HOUSE AT GRACELAND, guesthousegraceland.com

THE PEABODY MEMPHIS, peabodymemphis.com

BIG CYPRUS LODGE, big-cypress.com

DAY 5 **MEMPHIS**

- ★ Breakfast in Elvis' booth at the Arcade Restaurant
- ★ Orpheum Theatre
- ★ Memphis Area Transit Authority Vintage Trolley
- ★ See the Peabody Hotel Ducks march to their fountain
- ★ W.C. Handy House Museum
- ★ Memphis Rock and Soul Museum
- ★ Memphis Music Hall of Fame
- ★ Lunch or dinner at the Four Way

DAY 6 **MEMPHIS**

- ★ The Lorraine Motel–National Civil Rights Museum
- ★ Blues Hall of Fame Museum
- ★ Stax Museum of American Soul Music
- ★ Lafayette's Music Room
- ★ Memphis Gong Chamber

* Graceland
* Tigerman Karate Dojo and Museum
* Dinner at Earnestine & Hazel's

DAY 7 MEMPHIS TO CLARKSDALE

* Gateway to the Blues Museum
* Tunica Museum
* Lunch at the Hollywood Cafe or the Blue and White Restaurant
* Abbay & Leatherman
* Delta Dirt Distillery
* Muddy Water's cabin at the Delta Blues Museum
* Stovall Farms
* WROX AM
* Deak's Mississippi Saxophones & Blues Emporium
* Coffee break at Meraki Roasting Company
* Lunatic Fringe Luthiery

♥ WHERE TO STAY IN CLARKSDALE

SHACK UP INN, shackupinn.com

TRAVELERS HOTEL, stayattravelers.com/clarksdale

AUBERGE HOSTEL CLARKSDALE, https://www.aubergehostels.com/cdale

DAY 8 CLARKSDALE

* Hambone Gallery
* Cat Head Delta Blues and Folk Art
* A live music performance at Red's
* Lunch at the Bluesberry Cafe
* Riverside Hotel
* Dinner and live music at Ground Zero Blues Club

DAY 9 **CLARKSDALE TO CLEVELAND**

- ★ Hopson Planting Company
- ★ W.C. Handy Encounters the Blues
- ★ Sonny Boy Williamson II's gravesite
- ★ Emmett Till Interpretive Center/Tallahatchie County Courthouse
- ★ McCartys Pottery
- ★ Po' Monkey's
- ★ Mound Bayou
- ★ Peter's Pottery
- ★ The Devil's Crossroads
- ★ Dockery Farms

⚲ WHERE TO STAY IN CLEVELAND

COTTON HOUSE, marriott.com/en-us/hotels/memtx-cotton
-house-cleveland-a-tribute-portfolio-hotel/overview/

LYRIC HOTEL WEST END, choicehotels.com/mississippi/cleveland
/ascend-hotels/ms386

DAY 10 **CLEVELAND**

- ★ Cast of Blues and Mississippi Delta Chinese Heritage Museum at Delta State University
- ★ Grammy Museum Mississippi
- ★ B.B. King Museum and Delta Interpretive Center
- ★ Indianola Pecan House
- ★ Club Ebony
- ★ Charlie Patton's gravesite
- ★ The Peavine Railroad
- ★ Leland murals
- ★ The Birthplace of Kermit the Frog

DAY 11 **CLEVELAND TO JACKSON**

- ★ Winterville Mounds
- ★ Lunch or dinner at Doe's Eat Place, Blue Front Cafe, Big Apple Inn, or Hal & Mal's
- ★ Ethel Wright Mohamed Stitchery Museum
- ★ Mississippi Petrified Forest
- ★ Farish Street Historic District
- ★ Robert Johnson House

⚑ WHERE TO STAY IN JACKSON

HILTON GARDEN INN JACKSON DOWNTOWN, hilton.com/en/hotels/jantwgi-hilton-garden-inn-jackson-downtown

OLD CAPITOL INN, oldcapitolinn.com

FAIRVIEW INN, fairviewinn.com

DAY 12 **NEW ORLEANS**

- ★ Eagle Saloon
- ★ Frank Early's My Place Saloon
- ★ Singing Oak
- ★ Musical Legends Park
- ★ Coffee and beignets at Café du Monde
- ★ New Orleans Historic Voodoo Museum
- ★ The New Orleans Jazz Museum at the Old U.S. Mint
- ★ A show at Preservation Hall

⚑ WHERE TO STAY IN NEW ORLEANS

THE PONTCHARTRAIN HOTEL, thepontchartrainhotel.com

LE PAVILLON HOTEL, lepavillon.com

HOTEL MONTELEONE, hotelmonteleone.com

DAY 13 **NEW ORLEANS**

- ★ House of Sazerac
- ★ Louisiana Music Factory
- ★ Congo Square in Louis Armstrong Park
- ★ Saint Augustine Catholic Church
- ★ Music Box Village
- ★ Treme's Petit Jazz Museum
- ★ Backstreet Cultural Museum
- ★ Live music at Fritzel's Jazz Pub

"

Seems to me it ain't the world that's so bad but what we're doing to it, and all I'm saying is: see what a wonderful world it would be if only we'd give it a chance. LOVE, BABY, LOVE. THAT'S THE SECRET.

LOUIS ARMSTRONG

INDEX

ABOUT THE AUTHOR

AMY BIZZARRI is a Chicago-based author, teacher, certified sommelier, mermaid, and mom of two. When she isn't on the road in search of adventure, you'll find her in her vintage kitchen baking a cake from a vintage recipe or riding her bike along the Lake Shore Trail. Follow Amy's adventures at instagram.com/amybizzarri.